ANTARCTICA
Journeys to the South Pole

ANTAR

CTICA

Journeys to the South Pole

WALTER DEAN MYERS

SCHOLASTIC INC.

New York Toronto London Auckland Sydney
Mexico City New Delhi Hong Kong Buenos Aires

THE AUTHOR WOULD LIKE TO THANK THE ROYAL GEOGRAPHICAL

SOCIETY AND ROBERT STEPHENSON FOR THEIR ASSISTANCE.

ISBN 0-439-22003-3

12 11 10 9 8 7 6   11 12 13 14/0

Printed in the U.S.A.   40

First Scholastic paperback printing, September 2005

Designed by Kristina Albertson

To Michael and Spring Myers

Contents

ANTARCTICA

Journeys to the South Pole

Introduction

The crunching noise startled me from a sound sleep. I swung my legs over the side of the bunk and tried to figure out what was happening. Silence.

Then a few seconds later the noise came again. Louder. It sounded like something was trying to come through the walls of the ship.

"Don't worry about it," my bunkmate Peewee said. "The ship is ready to sink any minute and we're all going to be dead. No big deal."

Peewee had a habit of exaggerating things, but when he told me to go up to the top deck and take a last look around, I decided to go.

We had left St. John's, Newfoundland, five days before, headed for the northern end of Baffin Island above the Arctic Circle. My bunk was three flights down from the deck, and on the way up I reassured myself that Peewee didn't know what he was talking about. When I opened the hatch door to the main deck, I changed my mind. The sudden blast of cold air was an absolute shock, stopping me in my tracks. I tugged on my mittens as I tried to catch my breath. The mittens were designed for the cold weather,

ICEBERG NEAR LIVINGSTON ISLAND

big and cumbersome, with a special place for the trigger finger to poke through in case I had to shoot anyone.

I closed the heavy iron hatch door and squinted my eyes against the almost blinding glare. The blue-gray deck of the U.S.S. *Shadwell*, the ship I was on, was slick. I carefully made my way toward the ice-covered rail. As far as I could see, from the ship itself to the far horizon, the sea was filled with ice floes! They cracked and groaned and sometimes made a noise that sounded like a huge sea monster was trapped somewhere out there. The sound of the floes, as they moved against each other, and against the steel sides of the ship, was terrifying. That had been the sound that had awakened me.

The scene before me, the ice floes so close together that I couldn't see the ocean, was something I had never experienced before. But the numbing cold quickly brought me to reality from the fantasy in dazzling white. I was on a military mission taking supplies to a remote base within the Arctic Circle. In the hold of the *Shadwell* were huge crates marked with encoded numbers and smaller boxes with no markings that we weren't allowed to touch. Aptly enough, it was all part of the Cold War. To make matters even more interesting, there was a Russian icebreaker keeping a distant eye on us.

When we crossed the Arctic Circle I was in a world I had never seen before, a world of cold and ice and days that never ended. Before the mission was over and we turned south to head back to the United States, I would gain a new respect for the power of nature and for the explorers and adventurers who dared to risk the cold and ice at a time when nobody knew what to expect, and when only the wooden hull of a sailing ship stood between them and the elements.

The Arctic — relatively near to Europe and North America — is cold. The Antarctic is even colder. Today we know a lot about both of these remote regions. But there was a time when almost nothing was known about what we call the North and South poles. Studying the lives of the early adventurers to the Antarctic fills me with wonder and respect. These incredibly brave people not only had to find the places they imagined were there, they had to find ways of telling the world where the places were, and even to name them. The history of Antarctica's discovery and exploration is a truly remarkable story and a testament to human courage, persistence, and daring.

The Arctic was named for the constellation Arktos, "the bear," under which it lies. It is a cold, sparsely populated area that had been known since the late ninth century, but until the eighteenth century had not been extensively explored. Many early scholars guessed that Earth was more or less the same north and south of the equator. It was natural for them to call the bottom of the world the Antarctic.

What was in the Antarctic? Was it really just a mirror image of the Arctic? There were people, the Inuits, living on the fringes of the Arctic. Were there also a few tribes of hardy people living in the southern polar areas? Some people guessed that the Antarctic might be a temperate zone, with a climate mild enough to support an entirely new civilization. Others imagined a fantastic area populated by exotic beasts and semihuman creatures. Most people in the world didn't care one way or the other.

The Arctic region was hundreds of miles from most major European seaports and from the great naval powers such as Great Britain, Spain, and Portugal. The Antarctic region, on the other hand, was thousands upon thousands of miles away.

But if a new land existed, and if it was indeed possible to reach, there were still some who were willing and eager to find it. The reasons varied according to the imagination and interests of those who wanted to reach, or wanted their countrymen to reach, the far ends of the earth. For some, those interested in expanding the whaling trade for example, it was merely a business opportunity. For some, the lure of adventure was irresistible. For still others, the accomplishment of a major discovery would bring them worldwide fame and, if properly managed, fortune. But whether the attraction was purely commerce or the opportunity to serve their country while looking for new territories, many incredibly brave people were willing to risk their lives and fortunes to explore Antarctica and, ultimately, to reach the South Pole.

The technology of the day was increasing at a rapid rate. The fifteenth century saw the building of new, sleek ships, called *caravels*, capable of much faster speeds than earlier vessels. This alone raised the limit of what explorers could do and where they could go. British sailors were learning to eat lemons and vegetables to prevent the dreaded scurvy, which meant that they could stay on ships for longer periods of time.

But there was another factor, an excitement in the air, as more and more discoveries were being made. It became clear that the entire world would soon be known and might well belong to those who dared the most. In 1492, an Italian sailor by the name of Christopher Columbus had sailed from Spain across the Atlantic Ocean and discovered a new world. It was not the world he had intended to find, but it was new and exciting and had opened up an entirely new vista to sailors leaving European shores.

By the middle of the eighteenth century, Hernando Cortés had already sailed from Spain to conquer Mexico. Vasco da Gama and Bartolomeu Dias had sailed from Portugal and explored the west coast of Africa. Henry Hudson's ship, the *Half Moon,* had explored the east coast of what would become the United States, and Sir Francis Drake had already sailed from England to stake out claims throughout the world for Great Britain.

Not all of the explorations or new naval technology could be considered positive. Some nations wanted to conquer and exploit the New World that Columbus had discovered. And the slave trade flourished as fast ships were capable of taking their human cargo from the shores of Africa to the Caribbean and the Americas. Nonetheless, an exciting world was rapidly opening to explorers willing to dare the elements and set foot on unknown lands.

The Antarctic regions presented very special problems for explorers. In 1700, a trip across the Atlantic Ocean from Liverpool to Trinidad could take seven to ten weeks. A trip from London to the Antarctic would have taken seven to ten months.

The ship would stop to pick up fresh supplies along the way, but once the ship reached the frigid waters of the Antarctic, a new problem would emerge.

The Antarctic is surrounded by water, and in this incredibly cold area the water is frozen for most of the year. The wooden ships of the time, fragile by today's standards, could be easily ripped apart by the ice floes. They could also be trapped in the ice if the floes froze around them. Captains prepared as best they could, but no one really knew what to expect. Was the Antarctic simply a huge chunk of ice floating at the bottom of the world? Could there be people living somewhere in that foggy, difficult place? Were there vast fields of gold and silver just waiting for the courageous sailor to discover?

The history of Antarctic exploration is the story of nations eager to expand their territory into an unknown world, and of people of amazing courage, willing to risk their lives and property to discover the secrets of the fifth-largest continent on Earth. The story involves extraordinary navigators who would add to the scientific knowledge of the day, as well as ordinary sailors going about the business of making a living, not at all concerned about the meaning of their voyages.

But all of the early explorers, the seal hunters, and those on exacting scientific missions, dramatically increased the range of human knowledge. They also demonstrated a degree of courage and fortitude that reflected the depth, flexibility, and courage of the human spirit.

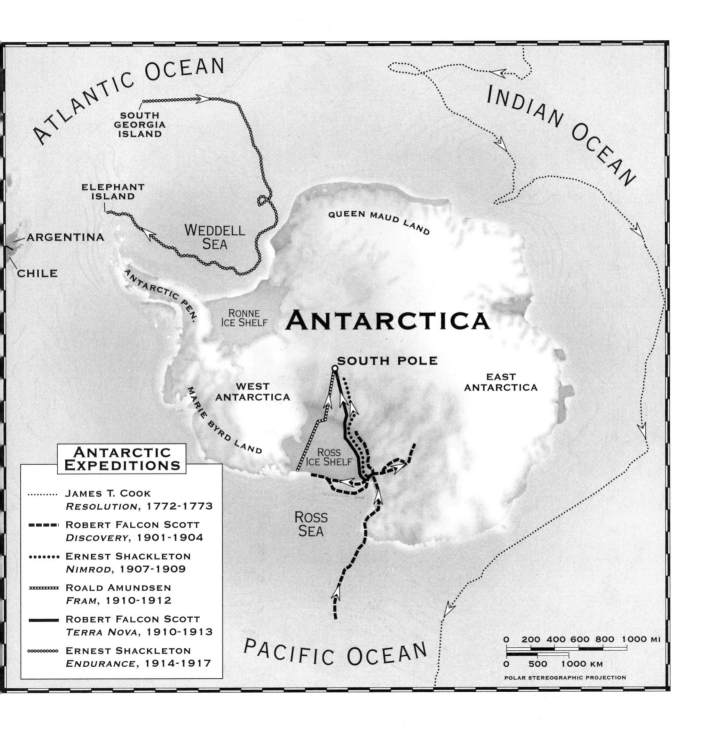

ATLANTIC OCEAN

INDIAN OCEAN

SOUTH
GEORGIA
ISLAND

ELEPHANT
ISLAND

ARGENTINA

CHILE

WEDDELL
SEA

ANTARCTIC PEN.

QUEEN MAUD LAND

RONNE
ICE SHELF

ANTARCTICA

SOUTH POLE

WEST
ANTARCTICA

EAST
ANTARCTICA

MARIE BYRD LAND

Ross
ICE SHELF

ROSS
SEA

PACIFIC OCEAN

ANTARCTIC EXPEDITIONS

.... JAMES T. COOK
RESOLUTION, 1772-1773

▬ ▬ ▬ ROBERT FALCON SCOTT
DISCOVERY, 1901-1904

●●●●● ERNEST SHACKLETON
NIMROD, 1907-1909

▦▦▦▦ ROALD AMUNDSEN
FRAM, 1910-1912

▬▬▬ ROBERT FALCON SCOTT
TERRA NOVA, 1910-1913

∞∞∞∞∞ ERNEST SHACKLETON
ENDURANCE, 1914-1917

0 200 400 600 800 1000 MI

0   500   1000 KM

POLAR STEREOGRAPHIC PROJECTION

7

A MAP of the SOUTH POLE, with the Track of his Majestys Sloop Resolution in Search of a SOUTHERN CONTINENT

Cape of Goodhope

AFRICA

dif. 1773

discoverd in 1772

Ice

Track in 1775

Islands

Ice

Much Ice

Much Ice

Sandwich Land

Antarctic Circle

Isle of S. Georgia

1775

South Georgia

SOUTH AMERICA

R. Plate

Valparaiso

C. Blanca

E Falkland I.

Streight Magellan

C. Horn

Staten

Patagonia

Chili

Ice Island

Ice

Ice

Ice Island

Ice

Track South Track in 1773

Antipodes of London

no Ice

no Ice

Cape

Dusky B.

NEW ZEALAND

Cook St.

X Cape

Track Fogg's Track Dec. 1774

Track in 1773

T. Bowen sculp.

Into the Unknown
James Cook Crosses the Antarctic Circle

When, in 1728, James Cook was born in Yorkshire, England, the entire world could have been described as "new" in the sense that most people had little idea of what life was like beyond the borders of their own country. Maps of the day would show Europe itself, the eastern coast of North America, the western coast of Africa, and only parts of what we now know as the Middle East and Far East. Could there possibly be great cities in central Africa? In the South Pacific? Was the bottom of the earth capable of sustaining human life?

There were many places on Earth where no Europeans had visited, even places where no human beings at all had visited. Scholars tried to guess what these places would be like. Some imagined monsters, or beings only half human, living in wildly exotic and scary lands. Others thought there might be wonderful areas with fertile soil for food crops and rich mineral deposits. But these were all guesses. To discover the reality, human beings needed to go to these places.

Cartographers, those who made maps, weren't sure how to represent these places. On maps the vaguely drawn lower regions of the earth were often labeled *Terra Australis Incognita*, "Unknown

MAP DRAWN BY CAPTAIN JAMES COOK

CAPTAIN JAMES COOK

Southern Land." Great Britain, the world's leading sea power in the eighteenth century, decided to send an expedition to these unknown lands. They chose James Cook to lead it.

James Cook was born into a farm family and might well have spent his life in the family business. But Cook was an exceptional youngster and, unlike most English boys of his time, was allowed to attend school until he was twelve years old. As a teenager, Cook became apprenticed to a man who owned a *collier*, a ship that transported coal, and soon found himself carrying cargoes of coal from northern England to the bustling docks of London.

Cook was ambitious and quickly learned that his ability to read set him apart from other sailors, even ones much older than he was. Ships at that time had none of the sophisticated electronics found on ships today. Instead, they found their way around the oceans using instruments that determined their position relative to the sun and stars. This took considerable skill. Cook read whatever books he could find on navigation and learned to use the instruments to find his position on the ocean. While the merchant ships he worked on carried cargo from port to port, James Cook assumed more and more responsibility as a navigator and learned the ways of the sea. Perhaps the greatest idea that he absorbed was that self-discipline gave one a huge advantage at sea.

After ten years on the collier, Cook decided to join the Royal Navy. The British navy was the most powerful in the world. Its officers were recognized not only as outstanding sailors but also as "gentlemen." For a young man born on a farm, it was decidedly a step up the social ladder. Again, Cook relied on his discipline and skills, thinking they would set him apart. He was right. Before long he was made a junior officer.

Cook, who had already taught himself a great deal about navigation, soon taught himself to draw accurate maps.

Cartography, the art of making maps, was a truly important skill. With so much of the world unknown, each time a ship left port, it was in danger of never finding its way back. A small error on a map, showing a body of land to be in one direction when it was not, could lead a ship hundreds of miles off course. Ships that needed to find sources of food or water could scarcely afford the days, and sometimes weeks, an errant map would cause them. But Cook's calculations were so well done, and so well thought out, that his reputation grew quickly. He was sent to the east coast of North America and directed to draw charts of the Canadian border, which he also did successfully.

In August 1768, the Royal Society decided to fund an expedition to the South Seas. It would be headed by Lieutenant James Cook.

Cook carried out the expedition, which was to chart the astronomy of the planet Venus from the South Seas. He did so successfully, using a converted collier, the *Endeavour*. During the trip, he also explored New Zealand and the east coast of Australia, which had never been visited by a European. Cook claimed the lands for Great Britain and drew highly accurate maps of the region. On his return to England in 1771, he was given a hero's welcome. By then, some geographers, people who studied the physical features of the earth, thought that there might be an undiscovered continent on the bottom of the earth.

In July 1772, Cook sailed from England in the sloop *Resolution* in company with the ship *Adventure.* His instructions were clear, to continue to explore the southern regions and to claim for Great Britain any new lands he discovered. When he said good-bye to his wife, Elizabeth, he knew it would be years before he would see her again.

Cook, now promoted to commander, sailed from England past France and Spain and down the west coast of Africa. His first major stop was at the Cape of Good Hope, which he reached at the end of October. As Cook left the Cape of Good Hope on the southernmost tip of Africa, he knew that no one had ever sailed across the Antarctic Circle, which was just over two thousand miles south of the Cape.

The nearer ships traveled to the Antarctic regions, the more difficulties they met. The weather became extremely cold and the winds less and less predictable. Since Cook's ships were driven solely by sail, it was easy for them to be caught in a storm and pushed hundreds of miles off course. As they approached the Antarctic regions, they would also find icebergs, huge chunks of ice driven by tides and the wind. If a ship hit one of them, a hole could be torn in the ship's wooden sides and sink it. In such a remote region, even minor damage to a ship would be a disaster.

In some places the ice did not rise high in the water but instead

LATITUDE AND LONGITUDE

Sailors had to figure out their positions by latitude and longitude. Latitude marks any given location on the earth relative to the equator. The imaginary horizontal lines drawn on maps above the equator are called north latitude, and those drawn below the equator are called south latitude. Latitude is given in degrees and minutes, with the equator being 0 degrees. The North Pole is 90 degrees north latitude, and the South Pole is 90 degrees south latitude. The Arctic Circle is 66 degrees 30 minutes north, and the Antarctic Circle is 66 degrees 30 minutes south. The distance between latitude degrees varies slightly, due to the fact that the earth is slightly flatter at the poles, but the average is about 69 miles per degree.

Longitude is the series of imaginary vertical lines drawn from the North Pole to the South Pole. To give these numbers a starting point, the vertical line that runs through Greenwich, England, was designated as 0 degrees. Longitude lines mark locations east and west of Greenwich, from 0 degrees to 180 degrees. The distance between degrees of longitude is the greatest (69.65 miles) at the equator; the distance between longitude lines decreases as the lines converge on the poles. A combination of latitude lines, crossed by longitude lines, form a grid that gives a navigator an excellent idea of where in the world he or she is.

formed miles upon miles of floating ice called "pack ice," that the ships would have to navigate through carefully. The captain of the ship would then have to weigh the dangers of going into the pack ice. If the ice froze over behind him it might be months or years before he could free his vessel. Sometimes the ice was simply too solidly packed to even attempt a passage.

When *Resolution* and *Adventure* reached 60 degrees south latitude, they began to see icebergs. They also began to have the problems that all sailors in the Arctic and Antarctic regions experience: intense cold, ice, and fog. Icy winds off the Antarctic could reduce the temperature by 20 or 30 degrees in seconds, literally taking the breath away. The *Resolution* was, like the *Endeavour*, a converted coal carrier. Around one hundred feet long, it carried more than ninety seamen and twenty or so marines. The *Adventure* carried about two-thirds of this number. Exact numbers varied due to illness, discharges, deaths, and desertions. The job of the marines was to

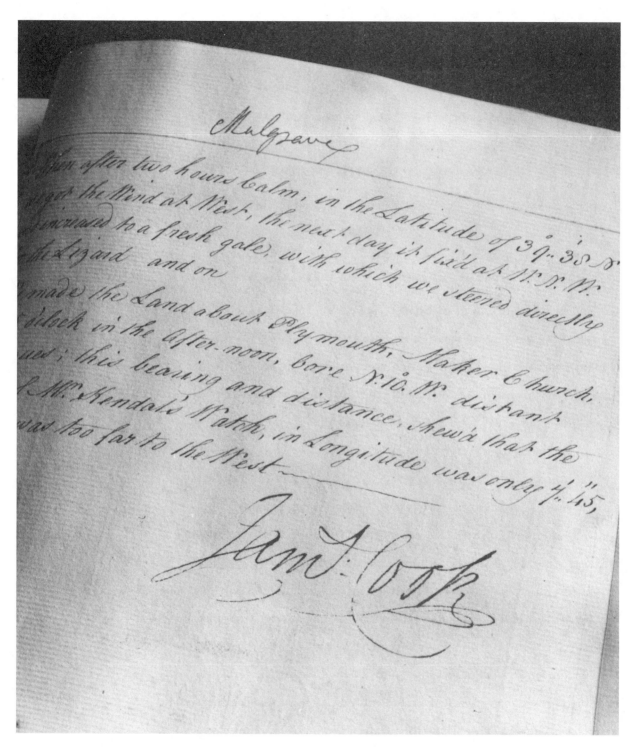

Mulgrave

... then after two hours calm, in the Latitude of 39°..38'..0"
... got the Wind at West, the next day it fixd at N.N.W.
... increased to a fresh gale, with which we steered directly
... the Lizard   and on

... made the Land about Plymouth, Maker Church,
... o'clock in the after-noon, bore N.10.W. distant
... ued: this bearing and distance, shew'd that the
... Mr Kendals Watch, in Longitude was only 4'..45",
... was too far to the West —

Jams Cook

CAPTAIN JAMES COOK'S JOURNAL

protect the ships if they landed on strange shores. They were also housed on the ships between the officers and the crew to prevent mutinies. The seamen were mainly young men, most in their twenties and thirties, some younger.

As Cook sailed south from Africa the temperatures began to drop dramatically. To climb up the ten-story mast with temperatures below zero and the wind blowing fiercely was hugely dangerous. Cook had to use all of his skills as a sailor to negotiate his way through the floating ice, keeping in mind that although the ship was being pushed by the wind, the ice was moved primarily by the current.

The fog was perhaps the most menacing feature of all. It could sit like a huge cloud on the water, engulfing large areas of the sea and obscuring vision for miles. Or it could appear suddenly, trapping a ship quickly and making the possibility of running into the ice an immediate danger.

The dangers of falling overboard were great. Sails were handled by men climbing up the ice-covered masts and clinging to ropes that were also covered with ice. Waves that splashed onto the deck would freeze before they could run off through the scuppers. Moreover, there was no cold-weather gear. Men would smear tar into their clothing to keep out the water, and wear extra clothing to fight off the bitter cold. But their hands were still exposed, and the grip on a rope or sail was extremely difficult. Sometimes the ice floes were so thick it would seem that, if a man fell overboard, there would be no place for him to land except the ice. That was lucky, for few men who fell into the waters between the floes survived the shock to their bodies.

In the extremes of the polar regions, when latitudes of 60 degrees or more are reached, the light is often bent in ways that are deceiving. Experienced sailors would misjudge distances or would see what they thought was land, only to find that it was just a huge iceberg, sometimes stretching as far as the eye could see.

Cook relied upon his skills and his crew and slowly pushed his way to higher and higher latitudes. He was in a place where no one knew what the weather was going to be like, but he had to judge whether or not the ice would freeze and leave him stranded. Any mistake on his part could mean the destruction of the ships and the death of the crew. On January 17, 1773, Commander Cook became the first human in recorded history to cross the Antarctic Circle, a fact he must have been pleased to record in his journal.

"On the seventeenth, between eleven and twelve o'clock, we crossed the Antarctic Circle in the longitude of 39 degrees 35 minutes east; for at noon we were by observation in the south. The weather has now become tolerable clear, so that we could see several leagues around us; and yet we had only seen one island of ice since the morning."

Cook had sailed in the east Antarctica region, some 1,650 miles distant from the South Pole. Not being able to penetrate the ice any further, he took his ships out of harm's way. He traveled to Tahiti, where his men rested until the next Antarctic summer.

COOK'S SHIP *DISCOVERY*

This time they approached the region from the west and sailed to a latitude of slightly more than 67 degrees south.

Cook sailed along the ice fields, looking for land, looking for signs that would tell him what was in the middle of all that ice. He moved inward again, this time reaching 71 degrees 10 minutes. The South Pole, at 90 degrees latitude, was approximately 1,200 miles away.

Cook sailed to South Georgia Island, which he named for King George III. He made observations about the island's location and how it looked. There were, he noted, thousands of seals on the island, as well as penguins.

Slowly, between the years 1772 and 1775, Cook and his men made their way entirely around the Antarctic region. They never landed on the ice or even determined whether there was land in the middle of all that vast sea of ice, but Cook had drawn the first truly useful maps and had put to rest all of the fables about there being a southern Garden of Eden or lush green fields. He honestly felt that no one would ever come to the region again.

He also showed what modern science and the use of navigational skills could achieve. James Cook expanded our knowledge of the world and of what brave people could endure. It was his belief that few people would follow in his footsteps to such a dismal and barren place. Cook, a man of enormous discipline, had fulfilled his mission, but he saw no reason why anyone else would need to explore the Antarctic. He returned to England in 1775.

Cook's third voyage to the Pacific, begun in 1776, had more

problems than usual. In New Zealand some of his crew members were attacked. They were also killed, and eaten. The encounter of Europeans with native peoples around the world was not going well at all. In 1779 in Hawaii, which Cook had named the Sandwich Islands, the natives took a small boat from the expedition. Cook retaliated by taking a local chief hostage. The chief's followers tried to rescue him, and in the ensuing battle James Cook was killed.

The official account of Cook's fabulous second voyage to Antarctica was published in 1777. At the time of its publication, England was at war with its American colonies. But Cook's accurate descriptions of the places he had seen, his exploration of the South Pacific and Antarctica, had advanced, as no one had before him, our knowledge of geography and the world. The plants and other specimens that had been collected from all over the world added immeasurably to all of science. Cook had gone where no man had gone before, and many of those who would follow would do so because of him.

Hard Work in the Frigid Cold

*C*aptain Cook's discoveries had been truly remarkable. He had forever changed the map of the world. All the fanciful theories of lush lands and exotic peoples that might exist in the world's southernmost parts had been largely put to rest by Cook's historic second voyage. Mapmakers, seeing Cook's charts of the Southern Hemisphere, published in 1776, hurried to their drawing boards. But the Antarctic was still the last region on Earth about which humans were still guessing. Was the Antarctic just a huge sheet of ice? If it was all ice, how thick was it? Could there be land somewhere in that frozen mass?

Cook's descriptions of what he had seen, all of his careful notations, did not paint a very promising picture of the region. In fact, he firmly believed that his expeditions would be the end of serious Antarctic exploration. If, as Cook suspected, no one could reasonably live in the region, and if there was no clear promise of precious minerals, why would anyone want to go there? For many years after Cook's last trip, he was correct. British interest in the Antarctic waned considerably, especially since at the time of Cook's death in 1779, the war between Great Britain and its American colonies was not going well. But Cook had drawn accurate maps and had described the region sufficiently to at least allow others to go and follow their own urge to explore. One of these men was William Smith.

Explorers are usually thought of as people who are interested only in the challenge of finding new places and reaching the most remote areas of the world — people who are spurred on by the spirit of adventure. But often great discoveries are made by those interested in the rather mundane pastime of making money. William Smith, an English captain, had commanded a whaling vessel. For years he had made his living hunting the huge mammals in the northern regions off the coast of Greenland. He had also done sealing. Both were difficult and dangerous jobs and in 1819, a full forty years after the death of James Cook, Smith was still working on the sea. By then he had given up hunting, for the somewhat less dangerous profession of taking passengers and cargo around the southern tip of South America. In 1816 Argentina had claimed its independence, followed in 1818 by Chile. Both countries were rich in resources but undeveloped. The only way to carry out trade was by ship along the coastlines and around the bottom of the continent at Cape Horn. What made the trip around the Horn, as it was known, difficult were the convergence of the currents and winds from the Atlantic and Pacific oceans. Violent storms were commonplace in the area, and hundreds of sailing ships were lost in this region as they tried to navigate their way from one coast of South America to the other.

Smith was rounding the Horn when he encountered bad

weather. He tried a more southern route, hoping to get out of the storm, but found himself being pushed much farther than he had wanted to go. Through the snow and fog, he was sure that he had spotted a land mass that was not on any of the maps he had seen. He noted the sighting in his ship's log on February 19, 1819. Smith made it around the Horn, and on his return to Valparaiso, Chile, he reported his findings to a British naval officer. He was not believed.

The weather in the Antarctic region is treacherous. Passages through the ice that are available to ships one season often disappear the next, depending on changes in temperatures. Smith attempted to find the land again in June of the same year, but was unable to do so. When he tried again in October, he was successful. He landed on what are now called the South Shetland Islands and claimed them for Great Britain.

"Claiming" an island or land meant that the person or expedition that first discovered the new territory could state that it belonged to whoever was sponsoring the trip or to the country of his citizenship. This idea led to countries claiming lands that were already "discovered" by the people living there. It also allowed the claimer to name the land. Smith called the islands he had found New South Britain. This name was later changed to South Shetlands because the islands were in the same longitude as the Shetland Islands off the coast of Scotland. Another likely reason for the name change was that the islands were not considered grand enough to carry the name of Britain.

SEALS

Crabeater Seals are the most common. They can travel on land at speeds of 15 miles per hour.

Elephant Seals can weigh up to 4,000 pounds and grow to 16 feet long. They were hunted primarily for their oil and were almost hunted out of existence. Once plentiful, it is estimated that there are fewer than one million left.

Fur Seals were hunted to near extinction in the nineteenth century. The seals, 4 to 6 feet in length, are making a slow comeback.

Leopard Seals are vicious. Often over ten feet long, and 800 pounds, they are the only seals that will attack and eat other seals or warm-blooded animals.

Ross Seals are shy. They have short faces and large, appealing eyes. Their fur is greenish gray. They grow to 7 feet long and generally weigh less than 500 pounds.

Weddell Seals grow to about 10 feet long and weigh up to 1,000 pounds. They can dive hundreds of feet deep and have been known to stay underwater for three quarters of an hour.

What Smith reported, and his crew verified, was that the islands were cold, windy, and wet. They were also covered with seals.

Whales and sea elephants were prime sources of oil. Ships would leave England or the United States and sail for months, even years, in search of this precious commodity. But there was a relatively new market in sealskins, which were sold chiefly in the Far East.

Seals were not acquainted with man and certainly knew of no harm that could come to them from these strange creatures arriving in their wooden ships. But come they did, with clubs and swords and guns, to trade in seal oil and pelts. Sealing was, at very best, a brutal business. The gentle seals sat passively on the beaches, and the men from the ships would go among them, clubbing them to death as quickly as possible. Hundreds and even thousands of seals could be killed in a single afternoon's work. Then the carcasses would be cut up, the skins would be separated and salted to preserve them, and the sealers, wading through the carnage they had created, would haul the dead seals to the boats. Many seal boats carried five thousand or more pelts plus tons of seal oil. Seal meat could also be eaten by the sailors and was a good source of vitamin C, although no one knew this at the time.

If European and American governments did not want to explore the Antarctic for scientific purposes, the sealers were more than willing to do so for profit.

When Smith had reported his findings, a small British-sponsored expedition under the leadership of Edward Bransfield was sent to the South Shetland Islands to investigate the sealing possibilities, to survey and chart the islands, and to formalize the land claims for Great Britain. Bransfield understood that it was necessary to keep the new source of seals secret for as long as possible. Accompanied by William Smith, Bransfield began his explorations and on January 30, 1820, spotted the mountains along the Antarctic Peninsula. This was the first recorded sighting of what would later be recognized as the Antarctic continent. Cook had never reported sighting any geological feature that would suggest the existence of land beneath the ice.

FUR SEAL ROOKERY

In the meantime, American sealers were also exploring the area. The best areas for taking seals were south of South America; both British and American sealers hunted for the rookeries where the seals congregated and bred. The Americans had an advantage over their British counterparts because they had found additional markets for their product. While the English took the seals primarily for their oil and found few markets for the pelts, the Americans had found a huge demand for seal furs in China. The sealers of both England and America were a particularly tough and hardy lot. Far away from restraining laws, they earned their pay according to what catch they made. Often they competed on the same beaches, killing seals in a bloody rampage while grumbling at each other. They also frequented the same taverns and ports when they were not working, so the American sailors soon found out about the newly discovered lands and its seals. In short order the "secret" of the South Shetlands had reached the commercial sealers of England and America. American sailors immediately sought to take advantage of what they saw as a new opportunity to hunt seals. Who claimed the land meant little to these men. Who could get the seals meant everything.

New theories about the continent began to form. The entire Antarctic region had been circumnavigated, or traveled around, and scientists were beginning to agree with James Cook that the land was too inhospitable to make it worth the while. The sealers, despite the loss of a number of ships, continued to ply their trade: It is estimated that in the years 1820–1822, over 300,000 seals

PALMER AND VON BELLINGSHAUSEN

One of the most daring of the sealers was an American, Nathaniel Brown Palmer, born on August 8, 1799, in Stonington, Connecticut. His father worked as a shipbuilder, and young Nathaniel and his brothers spent their days playing in the shipyards of this seaport town. Filled with stories about the sea and travels to exotic places, he dreamed of a career as a sailor. By age thirteen he was already working on a boat. In 1821 Palmer, then captain of a small boat, the 47-foot *Hero,* was sailing in the Antarctic regions, searching for new sources of seals. The idea behind Palmer's voyage was strictly commercial, and he carried no scientific personnel on his vessel. But as he hunted the seals, he pushed his tiny ship into areas that few, if any, men had ever visited. Palmer was barely twenty-one, sailing in a ship that most men would not have taken into the ocean, let alone the rough seas of the Antarctic.

Fabian Von Bellingshausen, on the other hand, was a career officer in the Russian navy. He had been chosen by Tsar Alexander I to lead the first official Antarctic expedition since the voyages of Cook more than forty years earlier. He left Russia in 1819 with two large ships, the *Vostok* and the *Mirnyy*. On February 6, 1821, he spotted a tiny ship just north of Deception Island. Surprised, he hailed her and went aboard. He was shocked to discover how young Captain Palmer was and that he had managed to achieve such southerly latitudes in so poorly outfitted a sealing vessel. According to an account written in 1907 by Palmer's niece and supposedly based on his journal, Von Bellingshausen asked to see Palmer's logs and, when he saw how extensive the *Hero*'s exploration had been, he named the area —which he thought he had discovered — Palmerland, in honor of the young American. However, since Bellingshausen does not mention this examination of the logs in his records this part of the story, which seemingly confirmed Palmer's reputation as an explorer, could be self-serving.

were killed. So many fur seals were destroyed that there was a real danger of extinction after only two years of contact with humans. Undeterred, sealers switched their attention to the larger elephant seals. Elephant seals were killed for the oil that could be extracted from their bodies. They, too, came very close to extinction.

With the depopulation of the seals, travel to the Antarctic

ELEPHANT SEALS

region dropped off dramatically. One of the most interesting sealing voyages, that of James Weddell, a Scottish navigator, explorer, and seal hunter, is worth noting. Looking for seals, Weddell found what he thought was a new ocean. What he did find was not a new ocean, but a sea, a smaller, enclosed body of water. On February 20, 1823, he reached the latitude of 74 degrees 15 minutes south, which was farther south than anyone had ever recorded traveling before. As far ahead as Weddell could see, there was nothing but open sea. There were some icebergs, which presented no immediate danger. Weddell had the benefit of those explorers and sailors who had gone before him: It was already the end of February and he knew the weather would soon worsen. He had already traveled nearly one thousand miles into the body of water that had been previously reported frozen. Wisely, he turned back, content to celebrate his high latitude. The sea he discovered has since been named for him, the Weddell Sea.

An interesting factor is that although the Antarctic is uniformly frigid, there are variations from year to year. Ships trying to navigate in the waters that Weddell found himself in, during the same time period, were met with solid ice long before they could reach 74 degrees latitude. It is estimated that the year in which Weddell sailed, 1823, the weather had been extremely mild. Weddell had found no important new sealing areas, but had explored an area that had not been investigated previously, and had left his record of his trips in a book, *A Voyage Towards the South Pole.*

Once the sealers had literally killed off their supplies, their explorations stopped. There are still disputes about who discovered what island in the region, or who first saw the mountains of the Antarctic continent. It could be that other sealers had landed on the continent and simply not recorded it. The sealers were, for the most part, excellent sailors, not explorers, and their major backers were commercial enterprises. Still, they did make a contribution to our knowledge of the area. It also became clear, as their stories were told, that a more scientific approach was needed in future explorations.

The Race Begins
James Clark Ross's South Pole Expedition

With the competing claims of who first discovered which territory or island in the Antarctic, a sense of competition began to develop between the nations interested in exploring these regions, as well as among the explorers themselves. One reason for the growing excitement was the fact that as each exploration was completed and written about, it provided more information for the next adventure. Also, the long trips were made easier by the discovery that cleanliness and lime juice could cut down on the illnesses of sailors. British sailors, issued limes to stave off scurvy, were given the slang name *limeys*.

But the major impetus for Antarctic exploration was science. In 1830 Michael Faraday was exploring the principles of electrical energy, and Charles Darwin was working on his theory of evolution. The possibilities of science were being advanced by new theories as well as new technology. The Royal Geographical Society was founded in 1830, and the British Association for the Advancement of Science was founded in 1831. Clearly, there was an explosion of interest in science and exploration.

The expeditions to the Antarctic areas were expensive, and often extremely dangerous. The justification for the expense was

SCURVY

Scurvy is caused by a prolonged absence of vitamin C. It's easily preventable, but when sailors were away at sea for long periods of time or in a desert area, such as Antarctica, it frequently occurred. It also is more common during periods of stress.

the collection of scientific knowledge. The Royal Geographical Society was very influential in securing government backing for such expeditions. The results were thought to be worthwhile, as nearly 25 percent of all of the varieties of plant life had been collected by expeditions exploring the south polar region.

The British, with the best and most experienced navy in the world at the time, and the most accomplished cartographers, seemed a likely candidate for further south polar exploration. It was the cartographers, those men who made the charts of the newly explored areas, who solidified the claims of the explorers. The Americans were undeniably bold, with the likes of Captain Nathaniel Palmer braving the ice floes in his sealing vessel, but his claims, lacking accurate logs and maps, were later disputed despite Fabian Von Bellingshausen's support of them.

Other countries were sending expeditions to the Antarctic as well. The Russians and the French had been the most successful. All of the ships had also been assigned the task of exploring the South Seas, and thousands of specimens were being collected for further study. When the British government decided to fund another expedition, the person chosen to lead it was James Clark Ross.

James Clark Ross, born in 1800, was only eleven years old when he entered the British navy. This was not unusual for the time. Boys of his age were often taken aboard British ships to be trained

SIR JAMES CLARK ROSS

for the sea. In America the usual stated age minimum was thirteen, but younger boys most likely found their way aboard American ships as well. Later in his career, Ross sailed with his uncle, John Ross, into the Arctic regions and in 1831, a month before his thirty-first birthday, he had arrived at the north magnetic pole. Compass needles always point to the magnetic poles and tell us where the earth's magnetic field is strongest. These areas are in the polar regions, but shift due to distortions in the magnetic field caused by irregularities in the earth's composition and other factors.

In 1839 Ross was given two warships, the *Erebus* and the *Terror*, with which to explore the Antarctic regions. The ships, already well constructed, were reinforced throughout to take the pounding of the ice against their hulls.

Ross was instructed to locate the south magnetic pole and to set up stations at which magnetic readings could be made throughout the year for scientific purposes. He hoped that the ice would be loose enough so he could sail most of the way to the magnetic pole. Ross read reports that both a French expedition under Dumont d'Urville and an American expedition under Charles Wilkes were also searching for the south magnetic pole.

Ross headed south, crossing the Antarctic Circle on New Year's Day, 1841. He encountered the same vast fields of pack ice that Cook, Bellingshausen, Weddell, and Palmer had met. But, with his reinforced ships, Ross began to push through the ice. It was a dangerous maneuver. Pushing through the ice one way was fine, if you were sure you could push your way back the other way. He was taking a chance that he would either reach land or, if the ice closed behind him, find another way out. Eventually, he came to an area of looser ice. Still mindful of the possibility of his ships being trapped, he continued forward, the heavy ice floes parting before the reinforced hulls.

Ross had to consider a number of factors. How strong were his ships? They had been reinforced to withstand the pressure of the ice and the battering, but would they hold up? How good were his crews? They were all volunteers and being paid twice the usual rate for the voyage. How much could he rely on the weather not to change and affect his charge through the ice? Ross calculated that he had a good chance of breaking through the ice and escaping unharmed. He knew that he had to keep weighing every factor, that if just one condition changed, he might have to turn back. He also knew that if he were wrong, his men would be trapped and most likely killed.

But Ross, like all those people who dare the unknown, was also willing to take a chance to complete his mission. Understanding that the two small ships were at risk, as were the lives of the crews, he pushed on. Eventually he broke through the heavier ice into a calmer sea that no one had found before. The sea would later be called the Ross Sea in his honor.

The Ross Sea, partially shielded from the frigid Antarctic storms, has periods during the year in which the ice is loose enough to sail through relatively easily. Given this chance, Ross turned his attention once again to the south magnetic pole. On January 11, 1841, a lookout reported a land sighting. Ross was doubtful at first, but as they drew nearer they saw that it was indeed land. This meant that they could not sail to the south magnetic pole but had discovered land farther south than anyone had ever been. The land was snow-covered and mountainous. Some of the mountains, which were at the northern end of the sea, were well over a mile high. Ross called them the Admiralty Mountains and the land on which they sat, Victoria Land, in honor of the queen of England.

Sailing westward through the Ross Sea, the two ships came upon an island he named Possession Island. He took a small boat to the island and planted a British flag, claiming the island for Great Britain.

Ross had a great deal of luck in his expedition. But the best of luck is useless without the rare combination of expertise and daring that he brought to his mission. He used his men well and his ships magnificently to bring them safely through the treacherous sea.

The next major discovery by this British explorer was an active volcano, which Ross would eventually name Mount Erebus, after his ship. The young botanist Joseph Hooker described the beautiful but bizarre scene of an erupting volcano in Antarctica:

"All the coast one mass of dazzling beautiful peaks of snow which, when the sun approached the horizon, reflected the most brilliant tints of golden yellow and scarlet; and then to see the dark cloud of smoke, tinged with flame, rising from the volcano in a perfectly unbroken column, one side jet-black, the other giving back the colors of the sun. . . ."

There was a smaller mountain east of Mount Erebus, which Ross named Mount Terror, after his other ship.

Captain Ross had still one more phenomenal discovery to make. Sailing in a southeasterly direction, he came upon the world's largest body of ice. Four hundred miles long and with a surface area nearly as large as Texas, it was a massive and stunning sight. It extended straight up from the sea some two hundred feet. Ross named it the Victoria Barrier, for England's queen, but it subsequently became known as the Ross Ice Barrier and now is known as the Ross Ice Shelf.

James Clark Ross was knighted shortly after his return to England. He had served his country well, claiming a greater portion of Antarctica for Great Britain than anyone before him, and penetrating closer to the actual continent than any other explorer. His exploits were soon known around the world, and few thought they could match him in daring or expertise.

In his lectures and writings, Ross made it clear that what he had accomplished had been in the name of the British Empire. The British, who had a proud record of exploration and the naval expertise to travel anywhere there were oceans, were undoubtedly the outstanding people in the field. But the British also made it clear, after Ross had returned and announced his discoveries, that they did not believe the claims made by some of the other countries, particularly those made by the United States and Charles Wilkes.

The Tyrant

Charles Wilkes and the First American Scientific Expedition to Antarctica

*C*aptain James Cook could be described as a great navigator, a great mapmaker, and outstanding in his concern for the health of his men. James Clark Ross was known for his daring balance of risks in completing his mission and also in seeing to the welfare of his crews. But Charles Wilkes, who led the first American scientific expedition to the Antarctic, was known as an absolute tyrant and the meanest officer in the navy.

Born in 1798, a year after the United States had launched its first major ships, Wilkes entered the navy as a young officer at eighteen. A thin, humorless man, he was chosen as an astronomer for an expedition to Antarctica in 1828. The expedition was canceled. United States naval policy was very conservative, and few Americans saw the need to equip and send ships thousands of miles to an unknown land. But ten years later, in 1838, there was more interest in sending ships to the South Seas and the Antarctic region.

One of the reasons was to "show the flag," to send a ship into foreign ports under an American flag to show the world that America did indeed have a navy and was a sea power that had to be respected. In the 1830s the fear of pirates was very real.

Unprotected American merchant ships traveling in the area of Tripoli were always in danger of being attacked. "Showing the flag" discouraged pirates and attacks on American vessels in foreign ports. American scientists also wanted to collect plant specimens and examples of animal life in the South Seas. Another, rather strange reason was the promotion of Antarctic exploration by retired army officer John Cleves Symmes. Symmes believed that the ends of the earth were hollow and that it would be wonderful if an American proved this. No serious American scientists accepted this strange theory, but they applauded his enthusiasm for exploration.

The United States might have thought of itself as a sea power in 1838, but it had little experience in putting together major expeditions. There were arguments about the size of the expedition and which scientists would accompany it.

When Congress finally approved funding for an expedition, the search began for someone to lead it. A number of naval officers turned it down, not seeing the value of such a trip and knowing that an expedition that did not achieve a great deal would hurt their reputations. Finally, the navy settled on Lieutenant Charles Wilkes, who had not been promoted in ten years.

Charles Wilkes was forty years old when the United States Exploring Expedition left port on August 18, 1838. Wilkes was a rigid man, high on discipline and not at all shy about sentencing a man to twelve lashes of the whip across his bare back. For what he considered serious offenses, Wilkes had ordered as many as forty lashes. His crews hated him and he knew it.

Wilkes began with six ships and a number of assigned tasks. He was to explore the vast South Seas, to look for commercial opportunities (seals, whales, fishing), and to find the south magnetic pole. The six ships started out with over four hundred sailors, officers, and a small group of scientists. The distinguished group of scientists had been assembled in the first major cooperative venture between the American navy and civilian scientists. The group included naturalists, a mineralogist, a conchologist to study shelled animal life, a philologist to study any new languages the expedition might encounter, a botanist, and two artists.

Wilkes gave each of his ships a different mission. One was to do charting, or mapmaking; others were to explore the islands in the Pacific; still others were to search for the south magnetic pole. One ship, the *Relief,* was sent home because it was too slow and could not keep in contact with the others.

The expedition reached Tierra del Fuego, on the southern end of South America, in February 1839. They sailed around Cape Horn toward Valparaiso, Chile, and on this leg of the journey one of the ships, the *Sea Gull,* simply disappeared and was never heard from again. This misfortune, the loss of a ship and its entire crew, was not unusual. These were sailing ships, dependent on the sails catching the wind to propel them over the oceans. The same winds, in the storms that raged around Cape Horn, were capable of sending them miles away from their routes or driving the ships into rocks or icebergs. The remaining ships on the expedition explored the coasts of Peru and Chile, and then went to Tahiti.

Fresh supplies were to be had at Sydney in New South Wales, Australia, so Wilkes took his ships there for a brief rest and to make necessary repairs.

In December, the day after Christmas, four ships of the expedition — the *Vincennes,* the *Peacock,* the *Porpoise,* and the *Flying Fish* — left New South Wales and headed even farther south. They reached the ice barrier on January 10, 1840. Wilkes writes:

"The 10th we encountered the first iceberg, and the temperature of the water fell to 32°. We passed close to it, and found it a mile long, and one hundred and eighty feet in height. We had now reached the latitude of 61°08'."

By the next day, the weather was changing quickly:

"We were all day beating in a thick fog, with the barrier of ice close to us, and occasionally in tacking brought it under our bow; at other times we were almost in contact with icebergs. During the whole day we could not see at any time further than a quarter of a mile, and seldom more than the ship's length. The fog, or rather thick mist, was forming in ice on our rigging."

Wilkes's sailors were interested in their new discoveries and what they might find. But they were also interested in survival, and at times that seemed unsure. Wilkes, in his report, describes his ship maneuvering through a field of icebergs during a storm:

"At 8 P.M. it began to blow very hard, with a violent snow-storm, circumscribing our view, and rendering it impossible to see more than two ship's-lengths ahead. The cold was severe, and every spray that touched the ship was immediately converted into ice.

"We found we were passing large masses of drift-ice, and ice islands became more numerous. At a little after one o'clock it was terrific, and the sea was now so heavy, that I was obliged to reduce sail still further: the fore and main-topsails were clewed up; the former was furled, but the latter being a new sail, much difficulty was found in securing it.

"A seaman, by the name of Brooks, in endeavouring to execute the order to furl, got on the lee yardarm, and the sail having blown over the yard, prevented his return. Not being aware of his position until it was reported to me from the forecastle, he remained there some time. On my seeing him he appeared stiff, and clinging to the yard and lift. Spilling-lines were at once rove and an officer with several men sent aloft to rescue him, which they succeeded in doing by passing a bowline around his body and dragging him into the top. He was almost frozen to death. Several of the best men were completely exhausted with cold, fatigue, and excitement, and were sent below. This added to our anxieties, and but little hope remained to me of escaping: I felt that neither prudence nor foresight could avail in protecting the ship and crew. All that could be done was to be prepared for any emergency, by keeping every one at his station.

"We were swiftly dashing on, for I felt it necessary to keep the ship under rapid way through the water, to enable her to steer and work quickly. Suddenly many voices cried out, 'Ice ahead' then, 'On the

weather bow!' and again, 'On the lee bow and abeam!' All hope of
escape seemed in a moment to vanish; return we could not, as large ice-
islands had just been passed to leeward: so we dashed on, expecting every
moment the crash."

～⬿～

On the 16th of January the four vessels were in the longitude of 157°46' east and land was sighted rising beyond the ice to the height of three thousand feet, and entirely covered with snow. It could be distinctly seen extending to the east and west of the *Peacock*'s position. Wilkes gave it the name of the Antarctic continent.

On the 24th of January, 1840, the *Peacock* was badly damaged as a gale pushed it backward into an iceberg, breaking the rudder

WILKES SIGHTED
ANTARCTICA ON
JANUARY 16, 1840

and steering mechanism. The boat's crew, unable to steer the vessel clear of the ice and fearing at any moment that the ship would be crushed, had to leave the *Peacock*, tie ropes to the other vessels, and then pull her out as they made their way over the floating ice. Somehow they freed her, and the ship started back toward Sydney.

The crews serving under Wilkes were tired and beaten down by their efforts. There were a number of ill men in the fleet, and the ship's surgeon suggested that Wilkes cut short the expedition, but Wilkes refused. He suggested that the men were faking their illness to embarrass him.

On January 30, 1840, the *Porpoise* passed the French expedition led by Dumont d'Urville. Due to a misunderstanding of their signals, the two expeditions passed each other without the customary acknowledgment of who they were.

Wilkes had started his expedition with 6 ships, 82 officers, 342 sailors, and 9 specialists. By the end of the expedition in 1842, he had discharged 62 of his men as unsuitable to serve in the American navy, an unusual action by a commander. There were 42 desertions — men who just could not stand serving under Wilkes — and 15 deaths.

On his return to the United States, there was more trouble. Wilkes's charts and discoveries in Antarctica were challenged by the British and questioned by the American navy. He was court-martialed for mistreating his crew, falsifying his log, exceeding his authority, and wearing the uniform of a captain while only a lieutenant. He was found guilty only of having men whipped beyond the accepted norms, a minor offense.

Wilkes remained with the navy and, as a captain in the Civil War, intercepted and captured two Confederate commissioners headed for England to solicit British support for the Southern cause. Because the ship they were on was a British vessel, the capture threatened the relationship between the Union and Great Britain.

Wilkes spent only sixty-nine days in Antarctica out of his nearly four years of exploring, but had surveyed nearly 1,600 miles of the coastline and had been correct in declaring the region a continent. During the expedition, his scientists had gathered thousands of examples of animal life, masks, weapons, and artifacts from everyday life that were typical of the South Pacific. These artifacts became the first major collection in the newly established Smithsonian Institution. Wilkes also produced a massive, five-volume report of the expedition, which added greatly to the knowledge of the South Pacific and of Antarctica. The Wilkes expedition, while little known today, was extremely important to the prestige and development of American science.

After the voyages of James Clark Ross and Charles Wilkes, interest in Antarctic exploration again waned. There was, of course, a great deal of interest on the part of individuals and the scientific community, but it had become clear that the difficult terrain of the land once known as *Terra Australis Incognita* required a great deal of money, probably from the government, if the explorers were to penetrate farther into what was now considered to be a legitimate continent.

Geographical societies, organizations designed to promote the advancement of our knowledge of the earth, were formed in several countries. In France it was the Société de Géographie de Paris, in Germany it was Die Gesellschaft fur Erdkunde, and in Great Britain, the Royal Geographical Society of London.

These societies brought together scientists, explorers, naval personnel, artists, and cartographers to create a framework for further study. Often government officials would be members of the society and important liaisons for funding. The societies became notably elitist, deciding among themselves whose research would receive money for further study and even whose ideas would get a public hearing.

After the expeditions of Ross and Wilkes, Europe found itself in a period of social and industrial upheaval. The rise of factory labor and the increased industrialization of the leading nations gave a different character to the average worker and a change in his social status that led to internal conflicts that diverted funds and interest.

In the United States the growing conflict between the industrialized Northern states and the Southern states with their plantations and system of slave labor also put support for Antarctic exploration on hold. For the next years the region was visited primarily by small ships hunting for seals or whales.

Exploration in the Modern Age

It wasn't until the end of the nineteenth century that Antarctic exploration began again. Two important expeditions of this era were a British expedition led by Carsten Borchgrevink and a Belgian expedition led by Adrien de Gerlache de Gomery.

Carsten Borchgrevink was born in Norway in 1864. On a Norwegian expedition in 1895 he had landed on Cape Adare, adjacent to the Ross Sea. He claimed to have been the first man to actually set foot on the Antarctic continent.

He then tried to raise money for an expedition that he would lead. He appealed first to the Australians and, when that failed, to the British. But when Borchgrevink appeared before the Royal Geographical Society (which it was called by 1895), he did not appear to be the kind of man the society wanted to invest in. The society realized that Borchgrevink, a rather rough and boastful man, did not have major exploring experience. Worse, he was not British, not well spoken, nor did he have the leadership background they were looking for. Borchgrevink said that he wanted to find the south magnetic pole, but the society, under the leadership of Sir Clements Markham, had a more ambitious plan. Markham wanted to send out an expedition that would do major

BORCHGREVINK ON
POSSESSION ISLAND

scientific work and that would also be the first to reach the South Pole. In short, an explorer in his own right, he wanted to create a British hero. He did not see Borchgrevink as that hero. Markham had someone else in mind, a rather obscure naval officer by the name of Robert Falcon Scott.

Borchgrevink, however, was determined to go on, and he attracted the attention of Sir George Newnes, a wealthy British publisher. Newnes provided a large sum of money for the expedition planned by Borchgrevink. Newnes, of course, wanted publishing rights to stories created by the expedition. The Royal Geographical Society was annoyed because the money could have been used to at least begin the funding of the society's larger expedition.

Borchgrevink purchased a Norwegian ship that he renamed the *Southern Cross.* The ship combined sails and a steam engine. The steam engine drove a propeller, which meant that, unlike on previous expeditions, the crew would not be reliant solely on wind. His stated mission was to land on the Antarctic continent, to actually spend the winter there, and to find the south magnetic pole.

The ship left London on August 22, 1898, stopped at Hobart, Australia, and crossed the Antarctic Circle on January 23, 1899. The ship could move without sails and therefore could maneuver closer to shore than ships with sails only, but there were dangers in pushing too far into the pack ice. As they approached Cape Adare the weather became bitterly cold. To see where they were going still meant sending someone high up on the mast, called the *crow's nest,* a difficult and dangerous job. Borchgrevink writes about it:

"All ropes and stays are covered with ice, your mittens stick to the ropes, and if care is not used you might lose your hold while the mittens are left sticking to the ropes. When you then try to avoid the danger by climbing without the mittens on, your hands get stiff and hard in a minute, and the chance of your dropping to the deck is greater than ever."

The *Southern Cross* arrived at Cape Adare (71° 17'S, 170° 14'E) on February 17, 1899. The landing party consisted of ten men and seventy-five dogs. This was the first time that dogs had been used as part of an Antarctic expedition.

The ship left two weeks later, and the small party of men were left on their own to try to survive the Antarctic winter. The ship would not return until January 1900.

The party explored the bay region as the days grew shorter. By the middle of May, the Antarctic night settled in and they were subjected to seventy-five days of darkness. It was depressing, cold, and nearly intolerable as raging storms dropped the temperatures to 35 degrees below zero. In October, one of the men, the naturalist Nikolai Hanson, died.

When the *Southern Cross* returned to pick up the men, they were in reasonably good shape. Although they had not accomplished much from a scientific point of view, they had shown that survival was possible even under the conditions of extreme cold and isolation.

Borchgrevink then tried to locate the southern magnetic pole. The ship moved along the edge of the continent, making several stops. On one stop Borchgrevink and two of his crew took a dog team ten miles south over the Ross Ice Barrier, reaching 78 degrees 50 minutes south latitude, a new record. He is also credited with the discovery that the Ross Ice Barrier is not stationary but moves gradually northward.

Borchgrevink's expedition added more to the science of the area, but his return to England was not greeted with enthusiasm. He was not part of the "inner circle" of explorers and scientists and was not supported by the Royal Geographical Society. He spent the rest of his life out of the limelight in Norway.

On January 19, 1898, the Belgian expedition, led by thirty-one-year-old Adrien de Gerlache de Gomery, entered Antarctic waters. The ship, the *Belgica,* was unusual in that it was equipped with a laboratory and carried an international crew of scientists and explorers. The *Belgica* was also unusual in that, unlike the ships that had gone before it, it had a steam engine as well as sails. In calm waters the steam engine could push the 118-foot craft forward at a speed of seven knots per hour. Among the crew members were Dr. Frederick Cook and a young Norwegian sailor, Roald Amundsen.

Success in Antarctica depended on careful planning, discipline, and luck. Often it was difficult to explain the successes of an

COMMANDER ADRIEN
DE GERLACHE

expedition or to tell exactly what went wrong. By the end of
February, the crew was beginning to have its doubts about
Gerlache and the mission as the expedition pushed farther and
farther into the ice floes. By March 3, Gerlache realized that the
ship's small engine could not get them out of the heavy pack ice.
Hopelessly trapped in the ice, they drifted for nearly a year, living
on fish and the ship's stores. One man died and two went insane.
They were able to begin the arduous process of cutting themselves

out of the ice in January 1899. But by then more than half of the crew was suffering from scurvy and depression. They did not free themselves completely until March.

Was the Belgian expedition a complete failure? Despite its troubles, it did make two notable discoveries: the Gerlache Strait and the Danco Coast. And two of its crew, Roald Amundsen and Frederick Cook, gained valuable experience and later would become famous for their own exploits.

HAULING SNOW FOR WATER SUPPLY ON THE *BELGICA* EXPEDITION

The Discovery Expedition

The driving force behind British interest in Antarctica was Sir Clements Markham, the president of the Royal Geographical Society. Markham wanted to launch a major Antarctic expedition that would, among other things, be the first to reach the South Pole. And he was determined that the expedition be British. He had actively opposed the 1898 expedition of Carsten Borchgrevink. Although the expedition had been called the British Antarctic Expedition, all but five of its members were Norwegian.

Markham had decided that British honor would be best served by having an expedition made up primarily of British subjects. In 1901 the Royal Geographical Society published *The Antarctic Manual,* a compilation of information and reports concerning the Antarctic. Markham himself wrote the preface to the impressive volume.

An interesting section in the manual was an article by Sir F. Leopold M'Clintock on the use of dogs in sledging operations. M'Clintock, who had used dogs in the Arctic, claimed that dogs could pull a relatively heavy load 25 percent farther than a man could, and a light load twice as far, without needing to stop and rest.

THE *DISCOVERY* CAUGHT IN SNOW AND ICE

The manual also included excerpts from the journals of John Biscoe, Charles Darwin, Charles Wilkes, and other explorers who Markham thought would be useful to the British expedition.

DOGS OFTEN PULLED SLEDS ON ANTARCTIC EXPEDITIONS

Markham then convinced the Royal Society, the leading British scientific body, to join with the Royal Geographical Society in raising funds for an expedition. The money was not easy to come by, but in 1899 Markham convinced a London businessman, Llewellyn Longstaff, to contribute a very large sum of money, and the project was on.

SIR MARKHAM WITH CAPTAIN SCOTT AND HIS WIFE, KATHLEEN

The choice of who would lead the expedition was also Markham's. In 1887, Markham had been in the West Indies, where he watched a boat race between young British sailors. The race covered two miles, from the starting point to a buoy and back again. It was an exciting race and Markham was impressed with the courage and stamina of the young man who won it, Robert Falcon Scott. He arranged to have dinner with Scott and clearly liked him. He also thought the young man would represent Great Britain well. So Markham followed Scott's career and, when the expedition was funded, chose him over many other candidates to lead it. Scott accepted the appointment, which, if successful, would greatly enhance his naval career. He also accepted Markham's idea that the expedition should exclude non-British.

The ship *Discovery* was built in Scotland especially for the expedition. It was a three-master made of oak, with a reinforced keel. It also had a 450-horsepower engine and a tendency to leak.

The *Discovery* left England on August 6, 1901. The ship stopped for supplies and necessary repairs in New Zealand, where the men aboard were treated as heroes. Markham had made sure that a public relations effort preceded the ship. By the beginning of January 1902, the expedition had reached the pack ice in the Antarctic region.

The *Discovery* cruised along the edge of the continent for close to a month, making observations, and making themselves familiar with the area.

In the beginning of February, Scott ascended in a balloon that had been supplied to him by the army. He went up some eight hundred feet in the balloon, which was attached to the ice barrier by a wire rope. It was not a good experience. The balloon strained at the rope that held it, bouncing Scott around in the basket. After Scott returned to Earth, a young officer on the expedition, Ernest

Shackleton, who knew a lot more about handling balloons, went up next and took photographs.

Scott understood his mission well, and recognized his own inexperience in polar exploration. But Markham had convinced Scott that he would not only become a celebrity but would also attain a prominent position in British history if he was successful. Scott approached each task carefully, and as a learning experience. He sent out several sledging teams and went on a number of journeys himself over the ice and snow. Most were useful trips in which the men learned about the area and took careful notes. But

BALLOON BEING DEFLATED NEAR THE *DISCOVERY*

on one sledging expedition a young sailor, George Vince, groping his way through a sudden blizzard, found himself slipping down a steep slope and then over a precipice. His body was never found.

During the winter it is all but impossible to travel safely in the Antarctic. The entire area is filled with steep slopes and precipices such as the one that claimed the life of George Vince. There are crevices, some three feet deep and others as much as six hundred feet deep, covered by a thin layer of snow, in which an unsuspecting explorer can fall. Finally, there are the winter blizzards and unyielding cold that threaten frostbite at any time.

The try for the South Pole was not to happen until the next spring. For the time being, Scott was content with setting up the station in which his men were to live and work, and setting up the scientific experiments that were an integral part of the expedition. The *Discovery* was anchored in McMurdo Sound, which Scott had found was not a lake, as previously thought, but a body of water separating Ross Island from the mainland.

To stave off boredom during the dark, cold winter months of April to August of 1902, a newspaper was put together by the men of the expedition, and edited by Shackleton and other crew members. Any officer or crew member could contribute to *The South Polar Times,* and many tried their hand at writing for the first time. Some of the articles were serious, others very funny, but it gave them all something to look forward to on a regular basis.

Finally the sun returned in mid-August, to cheers and relief. Scott immediately began to plan for the trek to the South Pole.

The shortest distance from the sea to the pole was eight hundred miles. Any journey would take months to the pole and months back, so there was little room for error. Food for the people and the dogs had to be carried with the explorers, and sufficient supplies left along the way for the return trip.

On September 17, Scott, Shackleton, and Michael Barne started out on a two-week trip toward the pole to check the route and to create a food depot. They ran into a vicious storm and the temperature dropped to 51 degrees below zero. They were forced to return to the ship after only two days.

A second, successful attempt to set up the depot was made September 27. Michael Barne, whose hands had suffered damage from frostbite, was replaced by Thomas Feather. The depot was set up with six weeks' provisions for the men and 150 pounds of dog food. The creation of this depot meant that the expedition, on the next trips, could set up other depots farther along the route; they would continue creating depots until there were enough for a team to reach the South Pole, and make it back.

Scott's attempt to reach the South Pole began in earnest on November 2, 1902. The three men who would make the trip were 34-year-old Robert Falcon Scott, 28-year-old Ernest Shackleton, and 30-year-old Edward Wilson. Scott and Shackleton were naval officers, and Wilson was a doctor, a zoologist, a very accomplished artist, and a man of deep religious leanings.

Scott and Wilson had become close friends. Scott was a career naval officer and an excellent organizer and leader. Shackleton was more of a rebel, physically quite strong, and very determined to complete any mission he attempted.

When the last of their support teams turned back, the three men with their nineteen dogs moved on with confidence. The trip had been planned carefully, and the three men felt ready for the hardships that lay ahead.

The scientific equipment, food supplies, tents, and other gear the explorers took with them were loaded onto long, sturdily built sleds. The dogs were harnessed to the sleds and driven by voice commands and a whip. Scott realized that none of his men had expertise in dealing with dogs, but he knew that they were necessary if the trip was to be successful.

The men understood that their exposure to the cold, and the constant strain of the journey, would exact a cost on their health and well-being. The longer they were on the trail, the more difficult it would be. When the progress of the first few days was less than they had hoped, some of their confidence waned. Scott knew that either the dogs were not performing as well as expected or the three men were not handling the dogs as well as they should.

On December 9, one of the dogs died. The others seemed sick and none of the small party understood why. When they reached the latitude of 80 degrees 30 minutes south, they put down a new food depot. But because their progress was so slow, they were forced to cut down on their rations.

By December 20, four dogs had died.

All three men were suffering from a degree of snow blindness, even though they were wearing goggles. Snow blindness is the very painful reaction of the eyes to the white glare of sunlight off the snow. But Wilson, the doctor, confided to Scott a new fear — that Shackleton was showing signs of scurvy. His gums were bleeding and his joints began to ache.

On Christmas Day, the men allowed themselves the luxury of a little extra food, including a plum pudding Shackleton had hidden away.

On December 27, they came upon a mountain with two peaks, which Scott named Mount Markham.

On December 30, 1902, they reached the latitude of 82 degrees 16 minutes, the farthest south that any human had ever been. But they had also reached their physical limits, and had to turn back. Wilson was suffering the most from the snow blindness, and Shackleton was coughing up blood.

By January 16, 1903, Shackleton was on the verge of collapse, and Wilson could barely see at all. The weaker dogs were killed to feed the stronger ones. It was a necessary action, but one that tore at Scott's feelings for the animals that had worked so hard for him.

On January 28, they reached the first depot, and on February 3, they were finally spotted by the lookouts at the base. The first assault on the South Pole had failed.

The *Discovery,* moored at McMurdo Sound, was unable to move in the ice. Scott tried to free her by blasting away the ice, but failed. When the relief ship *Morning* came with supplies, there were eight miles of ice between the two ships. Scott advised the captain of the *Morning* not to venture closer, lest it, too, be trapped in the ice. It was soon decided that the *Discovery* would winter over for a second year. Some of the original crew, including a protesting Shackleton, were sent home.

THE CREW OF THE
DISCOVERY

The *Discovery* expedition did more continental exploration than any previous group. Scott made other sledging journeys, most notably a long journey on the Ferrar Glacier. On this trip, at an elevation of nine thousand feet, they man-hauled four sledges. This meant that teams of men, with harnesses, pulled the heavy sledges themselves instead of using dogs. The *Discovery* was finally freed in February 1904, and in March, Scott crossed the Antarctic Circle on the way home.

Scott, a basically shy man, found himself a hero on his return and much in demand for speaking engagements and social events. He had not accomplished all that he wanted to in the Antarctic, but the stories he had to tell were still fascinating and the discoveries of his expedition undoubtedly valuable. Markham was disappointed by the failure to reach the pole but was sure that in Scott he had picked the right man and that it would only be a matter of time before there was a British success.

Ernest Shackleton and the Nimrod Expedition

$\mathcal{E}$rnest Shackleton had traveled with Robert Scott on the *Discovery*, accompanying the naval officer on the first British attempt to reach the South Pole. He had been bitterly disappointed at being sent home by Scott as a result of his bout with scurvy. By 1906, he was proposing his own expedition. He appealed to Sir Clements Markham for funding but was refused. He then decided to raise the money through public speaking engagements and appeals to wealthy British men and women.

There had been marked differences between Scott and Shackleton on the first expedition. Scott was a naval officer, a very careful planner, and a person used to being in full charge of his men. Shackleton, six years younger than Scott, had been in the British merchant fleet since he was sixteen. A strong and determined man, he did not get along very well with Scott and, in fact, thought that Scott had made some bad decisions on the first expedition.

Shackleton felt that he knew why the first try for the pole had failed. The trek from the base camp to the pole would take weeks, and food and supplies were needed both to reach the pole and to return. The difficulty was in the men dragging the supplies over

MANCHURIAN PONIES USED TO PULL SLEDS BY SHACKLETON

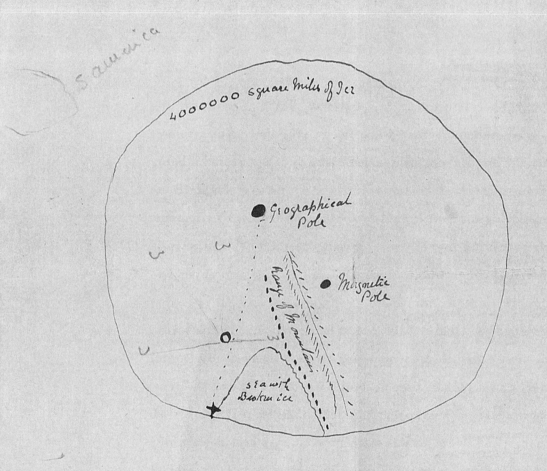

S america

4000000 square miles of Ice

Geographical Pole

Magnetic Pole

Range of mountains

Sea with Broken ice

New Zealand.

Ponies dogs & Motor Car

o Camping ground for 5 months in hut with 12 men, quite dark with temp 60 degrees Below Zero
+ Starting place of expedition
..... proposed route
------ Capt Scott expedition

the ice and through the blizzards and freezing temperatures. Each day the men had grown more and more tired, the wear on their bodies becoming nearly unbearable.

Shackleton planned to bring a 15-horsepower Arrol-Johnston automobile, a team of Manchurian ponies, and trained sledge dogs. Even if the automobile, the ponies, and the dogs failed to get him and his men all the way to the pole, at least the men would be in better shape than if they had to pull the heavy loads all the way.

Shackleton had also had disagreements about the men Scott had selected. He felt that Scott had picked people he liked, with less regard than he should have had for their qualifications to make such a hard trip. Where Scott wanted "team players," Shackleton wanted individuality. He wanted people he could get along with, but he was more interested in physical and emotional strength.

When Scott heard that Shackleton was planning his own expedition, he was annoyed. He was even more bothered to discover that the man he had sent home with scurvy years before was planning to use Scott's own base. He contacted Shackleton and asked him not to use his base because Scott was planning a second expedition of his own. The two men agreed that Shackleton would set his base on the barrier to the east.

The *Nimrod* was an old but sound ship that had been used in sealing operations. Necessary repairs were quickly done, and on August 7, 1907, the *Nimrod* left England on its way toward the Antarctic. After a stop in New Zealand, where he did more fund-raising, Shackleton reached the Antarctic in January 1908.

A SKETCH OF HIS PLANNED ROUTE BY SHACKLETON

MEMBERS OF THE
SOUTHERN PARTY
INCLUDING SHACKLETON,
SECOND FROM LEFT.

But when he neared his planned landing spot, he found that tons of ice had broken from the ice shelf and blocked his entrance. He continued to search for a good landing spot and finally moored twenty miles north of Hut Point, the location used by Scott, which Shackleton had promised not to use.

The hut Shackleton's crew built was 33 feet by 19 feet, and 8 feet high. Fifteen men were to live in the hut over the winter, setting up scientific experiments and preparing themselves for the try for the pole in the spring. The winter went slowly, with the men trying to relieve the boredom of living away from their families and friends. They had a phonograph, but the records, played over and over, soon became boring. There were also jobs to be done. Ice had to be cut so that it could be melted down for water, and the ponies had to be cared for on a daily basis. Inside the hut the temperature was usually only 20 to 30 degrees. Many of the men slept in their clothing. Anyone taking a bath had to do it quickly before the water froze.

In September a three-man party, Douglas Mawson, A. F. Mackay and E. Davis, started out for the south magnetic pole. Two of the

INSIDE ONE OF THE WINTER HUTS

men were Australian and the third a British naval surgeon. They first rode in the automobile, setting out depots short distances from the base. After the automobile quickly broke down, the men figured the distance they would have to walk, counting planned detours around mountainous areas, as roughly a thousand miles, pulling three hundred pounds of food and equipment. Averaging about 8.5 miles per day, they reached the south magnetic pole, where the needle of the compass stood vertically, in mid-January 1909.

Once they had reached the south magnetic pole, they needed to find their way back before their supplies ran out. It was an extraordinarily hard trip back, and they sighted the *Nimrod* just as one of the three, Douglas Mawson, fell into a twenty-foot-deep crevasse, a crack in the ice that was covered by a thin layer of ice

AUTOMOBILE USED DURING THE *NIMROD* EXPEDITION

MAGNETIC POLE

The earth has its own magnetic field that can be detected with a compass. The ends or "poles" of the field are found in the Arctic and Antarctic regions but not at the same place as the geographical poles that represent the earth's extremes of north and south. The north geographical pole is about eight hundred miles from the northern magnetic pole. The south geographical pole is about sixteen hundred miles from the south magnetic pole.

and snow. Luckily, a rescue party from the *Nimrod* came out and was able to pull the exhausted explorer from the ice.

The next goal was the geographic South Pole. To travel the hundreds of miles from the edge of the ice where they had formed their base camp to the geographic South Pole, Shackleton and his crew had to carry a three-month supply of food for the men and animals, and had to ration it carefully. The party started out on October 29, with enough food for ninety-one days. They took pemmican, wheat-meal crackers, sugar, cheese, and chocolate. Pemmican was the staple food in polar work and was made of powdered beef, fat, and other ingredients. This was mixed with melted snow and whatever meat was available to make a stew referred to as "hoosh." Within days the men felt the need for more food than they were getting, and within a few weeks they were constantly hungry and thinking of food.

On November 21, they killed the weakest pony, ate part of its flesh, and left the rest for the return trip.

One of the men developed a bad tooth and it was pulled with some rough tools the surgeon had brought along.

Two more ponies were shot and the last one fell into a crevasse. When the men looked into the crevasse, they could see nothing but a bottomless black hole. The men began to eat the maize they had brought to feed the ponies.

On Christmas Day they realized they were still about 250 miles from the pole. Could they reach it? And if they did, could they make it back?

The weather, always miserably cold, turned worse. For several days they had to lie in their tents, unable even to stand for long periods against the driving blizzard.

On January 9, 1909, after having traveled farther south than any other human beings, and coming within a hundred miles of the South Pole, they turned back. To turn back meant defeat: they had not achieved their goal of reaching the South Pole. But turning back gave them a chance to survive. On January 27, nearly out of food, they reached a depot. On February 13 they reached the depot where they had left a dead pony and ate parts of it. They finally reached the *Nimrod* on March 3.

Shackleton's small party had set a "furthest South record," surpassing Scott's record and establishing himself as a British hero. Even though he had not reached the pole, when he returned to England it was as a celebrity. After a brief time with his family, Shackleton began lecturing on his experiences. Public clubs and private parties were eager to invite him to talk about his exploits. He changed the way he dressed, adopting more formal wear, and accepted with pride the idea that his picture was prominently displayed in the London papers. But he dreamed of another expedition.

In the meantime, Scott, with the backing of Sir Clements Markham, also began planning another expedition. There was no doubt that someone would reach the South Pole, and with more and more experience, it would probably happen soon. The race was heating up, and Robert Falcon Scott was ready for it. But there were others planning as well.

SHACKLETON NEXT TO HIS FLAG AFTER REACHING FURTHEST SOUTH

On the Ground
in Antarctica

In September 1909, newspapers announced that an American explorer, Robert E. Peary, had reached the North Pole. This was stunning news. Explorers who had wanted to be the first to reach a geographic pole had only one option now, and that was in Antarctica. The two main players in what was to become the most exciting race in history were the Norwegian Roald Amundsen, who had been on the *Belgica,* and Robert Falcon Scott, who had led the Royal Society Expedition of 1901–1904.

Besides the sheer adventure, these men were on a quest for fame, knowing full well that the first to reach the pole would have his name remembered forever. In 1910 Robert Falcon Scott set sail from England to join the crew of the *Terra Nova* to travel to Antarctica. His mission, to be the first to reach the South Pole.

Scott, in his early forties, was confident of his abilities and those of his carefully selected team. There was a scientific mission to be carried out as well as reaching the pole, but there was no doubt that the pole was Scott's primary mission as he traveled southward.

In September, he received a disturbing telegram. It read,

The crew of the *Terra Nova* eating

simply, BEG LEAVE TO INFORM YOU, *FRAM* PROCEEDING ANTARCTIC. It was signed by Roald Amundsen.

The meaning was clear. Amundsen was intending to race Scott to the South Pole. Scott was incensed. Amundsen's mission had no scientific pretense, no higher purpose than being the first to reach the pole. In an instant Scott's entire life and reputation were at stake. The team that reached the pole first would be recorded forever in the annals of exploration. Everyone else would be followers.

Amundsen also knew this. In a way, he had no choice but to challenge Scott. He knew that Scott was a capable man, and that the British had already come close to reaching the pole. He knew his decision would not be popularly accepted in the exploration community, because he had changed the rules of the exploring game. He had taken away the idea that exploration was primarily a scientific endeavor and turned it into an exciting but dangerous race for glory.

Scott also knew who Amundsen was. The *Belgica* voyage had been well publicized, and Amundsen also had achieved fame by his discovery of the Northwest Passage, the route from the Atlantic to the Pacific ocean through northern Canada.

Amundsen had prepared well for the trip. He worked on his equipment, consulting with experts in arctic travel. He very carefully assembled a crew of highly competent men for the final push. Olav Bjaaland was a champion skier who would choose the

CAPTAIN SCOTT

equipment and advise the other men, all skiers in their own right, about the problems they might encounter.

Helmer Hanssen was a dog expert and deputy leader.

Oscar Wisting was a whaler, tough as nails, Amundsen's closest friend, and a man dedicated to making the expedition a success.

Sverre Hassel was a man who could fix anything, from harnesses to bulky sledges. If a blade needed to be sharpened, he could do it. If a leather strap needed repair, Hassel was the man for the job.

While Amundsen's plan involved a major element of speed, Scott's did not. Scott's plan was to focus on science, with speed being a secondary consideration. Amundsen's sole focus was speed. With Amundsen already on his way, it was too late for Scott to redesign his mission.

Amundsen was convinced he could beat Scott to the pole because he knew that the British expeditions were extremely limited in their use of dogs.

AMUNDSEN WITH THE *FRAM* IN THE BACKGROUND

Sledge dogs are of no special breed, but have a natural inclination to pull when they are harnessed. Usually weighing forty to fifty pounds, a dog can pull ten times his own weight for a good distance. A team of six to eight dogs can run for hours pulling hundreds of pounds on a sledge. But it took months to train dogs and even longer to become expert enough to make them useful. The British expedition did not have the expertise required for speed, and Scott knew it as well as Amundsen. But although he had little hope of beating Amundsen, there was no turning back. He had dogs with him, and nineteen Siberian ponies, but Scott was going to again rely on himself and his chosen men to haul the heavy sledges to the pole. The ponies were not Scott's ideal. He knew they would be trouble, but he also knew, from his first expedition and from Shackleton's efforts, that he could not handle dogs. In fact, Scott had written in one of his diaries that he had completely lost faith in the animals.

THE PONIES SCOTT'S TEAM BROUGHT TO THE SOUTH POLE

Man-hauling hundreds of pounds across the ice for days is an exhausting task. Teams of dogs or ponies can pull the same weight with relative ease.

Scott, in the *Terra Nova,* reached his starting point in January 1911. He immediately started building his winter quarters and began the process of putting out depots of supplies. He had twenty-six dogs, eight ponies, and three motor sledges. One of the sledges went through the ice shortly after it was unloaded, but the other two were useful for most of the year at the beginning of their polar journey before breaking down. The progress was slow and by early March six of the ponies were dead.

THE DECK OF THE *TERRA NOVA*

Amundsen, in the *Fram,* a ship given to him by a fellow Norwegian, polar explorer Fridtjof Nansen, reached his starting point on January 15 and began laying his depots on February 10, using three sledges and eighteen dogs. The laying of supplies went well and he laid them out carefully, building "cairns," mounds of ice to serve as markers so they could find the supplies again.

The drive to the pole could not begin until the short Antarctic summer (November to February), so both parties spent the winter at their bases waiting to begin the race. In June in the heart of the Antarctic winter, three men from Scott's party — Edward Wilson, a naturalist, Henry Bowers, a naval officer, and Apsley Cherry-Garrard, an English adventurer who had bought his way onto the expedition — went searching for penguin eggs and barely made it back to the base.

Amundsen, thinking he might need even more speed, had his sledges rebuilt, cutting their weight from 165 pounds to under 50 pounds each. He could do this because his supply depots were so well stocked that the sledges would not have to carry as much food. He also planned to use some of the dogs as food.

Amundsen first started toward the South Pole on September 8, 1911. He reached only 80 degrees south latitude when the temperature, which had dropped to 68 degrees below zero, turned him back.

He began again around October 19, with fifty-two dogs, four sledges, and five men. The men were all excellent skiers and had experience handling dogs.

By October 26 they had passed the first depot. By November 5 they had passed 82 degrees south. Amundsen noted that the dogs were pulling an average of only eighty pounds. The men were either riding the sledges or being pulled behind them.

On the first of November, Robert Scott started his trek to the pole with ten ponies, two dog teams and a five-man team that would go for the pole. A support team went with them, carrying supplies and returning to the base as Scott ordered. Accompanying Scott on the final try for the pole were Edward Wilson; Henry Bowers; Laurence Oates, a soldier who had paid his way onto the expedition; and Edgar Evans, another military man.

By November 17 the Norwegians, with very little difficulty, had reached the Transantarctic Mountains at 85 degrees south. They had trouble climbing up a glacier they encountered; but by December 7 they had reached 88 degrees south, only two degrees from the pole.

On December 10 the Scott party reached the Beardmore Glacier at 84 degrees. By then, all of the dogs and ponies were dead. The men were still nearly five hundred miles from the pole and were man-hauling the sledges through intensely cold weather and storms.

Six days later, on December 16, Amundsen and his team reached the pole. The race was over. Over the next two days they took sightings to verify their position and left markers. They also left a Norwegian flag lashed to a tent, a pennant bearing the name *Fram*, some gear, and letters to the king of Norway and one for Scott.

Roald Amundsen (left) and three of his men at
the South Pole, Dec. 16th, 1911.

They began their return journey on the eighteenth, reaching their base on January 26, 1912.

On January 16, 1912, the Scott party, exhausted and suffering from frostbite and scurvy, neared the pole, only to see evidence that Amundsen had been there before them.

"Tuesday, January 16. — Camp 68. Height 9760. T. -23.5°. The worst has happened, or nearly the worst. We marched well in the morning and covered 7¹/₂ miles. Noon sight showed us in Lat. 89°42' S., and we started in high spirits in the afternoon, feeling that tomorrow we should see us at our destination. About the second hour of the march Bowers' sharp

eyes detected what he thought was a cairn; he was uneasy about it, but argued that it must be a sastrugus. Half an hour later he detected a black speck ahead. Soon we knew that this could not be a natural snow feature. We marched on, found that it was a black flag tied to a sledge bearer; nearby the remains of a camp; sledge tracks and ski tracks going and coming and the clear trace of dogs' paws — many dogs. This told us the whole story. The Norwegians have forestalled us and are first at the Pole. It is a terrible disappointment, and I am very sorry for my loyal companions."

Scott had found what he must have suspected all along, that Amundsen had beaten him to the pole. To have reached the South Pole now became an anticlimax, a footnote in the history of exploration instead of the headline he had so hoped for. The men lined themselves up and took a photograph to mark the occasion. Then they had to begin the arduous journey back.

The journey back to their camp and safety would be eight hundred grueling miles. Scott, crushed by disappointment, still tried to make the most of his trip back. The men were growing desperately weak. There were clear signs of scurvy.

On February 8 and 9, fighting the depression that gripped the entire team, they collected rock specimens to carry back. By February 11 they were low on food and were unsure of their direction.

"Saturday, February 17. . . . seeing Evans a long way astern, I camped for lunch. There was no alarm at first, and we prepared tea and our

own meal, consuming the latter. After lunch, and Evans still not appearing, we looked out to see him still afar off. By this time we were alarmed and all four started back on ski. I was the first to reach the poor man and shocked at his appearance; he was on his knees with clothing disarranged, hands uncovered and frostbitten, and a wild look in his eyes. . . . He died quietly at 12:30 A.M."

Evans was the first to die. It would get worse as the remaining men, growing weaker by the hour, struggled through Antarctic storms.

On March 17, suffering from frostbite and scurvy and realizing that he would not make it back, Oates made a decision: "I am just going outside and may be some time." They all knew he was dying, and when he left the tent that cold day on his birthday, they let him go. He was never seen again. He was the second to die.

On March 19, Scott realized that his frozen foot would have to be amputated. Ten days later he wrote a final note.

ONE DAY'S SLEDGING RATION FOR ONE MAN FROM THE *TERRA NOVA* EXPEDITION

"Thursday, March 29 — Since the 21st we have had a continuous gale from W.S.W. and S.W. We had fuel to make two cups of tea apiece and bare food for two days on the 20th. Every day we have been ready to start for our depot 11 miles away, but outside the door of the tent it remains a scene of whirling drift. I do not think we can hope for any better things now. We shall stick it out to the end, but we are getting weaker, of course, and the end cannot be far.

It seems a pity, but I do not think I can write more.

     R. Scott

Last entry.

For God's sake look after our people."

By then, everyone in Scott's desperate little party had died. They had not become the first to reach the South Pole, and had died miserably and alone thousands of miles from home. They were found some eight months later, on November 12, 1912, by a search party from the base camp. Around them were their diaries, records, and thirty-five pounds of geological specimens.

The Unforgiving
Antarctic

The world was still awaiting news of the attempts on the South Pole by Roald Amundsen and Robert Falcon Scott when the Australasian Antarctic Expedition began in December 1911. The expedition was led by Douglas Mawson, an experienced explorer who had sailed with Ernest Shackleton on the *Nimrod*. Now, with a party of scientists from Australia and New Zealand, he proposed to explore the coastal areas of the continent. Among the innovations he would introduce were the use of an airplane engine to pull the sledges, and the first radios in the Antarctic.

The team set up a base at Cape Denison in January 1912 and quickly discovered that they were in one of the windiest places on Earth. The winds were routinely forty to fifty miles an hour. Setting up their huts and equipment was extremely difficult, but by the end of the month they had succeeded. In August and September, they attempted to set up supply depots, but in October the weather turned bad again, keeping the men in their huts.

The first sledging party, made up of Mawson, Dr. Xavier Mertz, and B.E.S. Ninnis, started pushing southeastward in November. They had spent some time trapped in an ice cave by the weather but were finally on the move again with three sledges. On

December 6, they were stopped again by the weather, with driving winds that reached seventy miles per hour, for three days. On December 13, they combined their equipment onto two of the sledges. The next day the wind was not quite as bad. They moved fairly easily across a terrain that was treacherous because of its crevasses — deep cracks in the ice — often difficult to see because they were covered by snow. Mertz, a skiing champion, spotted a crevasse and pointed it out. Mawson, driving one of the sledges, crossed it without incident, but then Mertz cried out in panic. Mawson brought his dog team to a quick halt and turned back. There was nothing behind him, no sign of Ninnis, the army lieutenant.

Mawson and Mertz went back to the crevasse, approaching the edge carefully. They looked down and saw one dog on a ledge. The dog, which had fallen over a hundred feet, was clearly injured. Beyond the dog, there was nothing except the darkness of the hole.

There was no doubt that Ninnis was dead, or dying. With him were the six strongest dogs, the dog food, the tent the team depended on, and most of the men's food. Mawson examined their remaining supplies and saw that, with careful rationing and not feeding the dogs, they had enough food to last ten days. They were 315 miles from their nearest supplies and had no radio with them.

The only available food were the dogs, and the men began to kill them. Mertz ate the dogs' livers and became extremely tired. The two men had to find more supplies, and quickly. On Christmas Day, Mawson and Mertz were 160 miles from their base, and Mertz was not doing well. On New Year's Day, 1913, Mertz developed stomach pains. He died on January 7. It was later determined that Mertz had died from vitamin A poisoning from eating the dogs' livers. Mawson was now alone. He wrote in his journal.

"For hours I lay in the bag rolling over in my mind all that lay behind and the chance of the future. . . . My physical condition was such that I felt I might collapse at any moment. . . . Several of my toes commenced to blacken and fester near the tips and the nails worked loose."

On January 11, the soles of Mawson's feet came loose and he had to bandage them back on. His body was now sore all over and his hair was falling out. Six days later, he fell into a crevasse, catching himself at the end of his rope. He pulled himself to the top, then fell back. Again he pulled himself to the top, this time throwing his feet up first and dragging himself to the surface. He kept going, making less and less progress each day. But on January 29, he spotted a cairn that had been built by a search party from the expedition. There was food and a note that they were waiting for the three men to return. The note also fixed the location of the ice cave as being only twenty-three miles away. Mawson reached the cave on February 1. When Mawson finally reached camp, he saw the *Aurora* leaving in the distance. The realization soon set in that he would have to winter over in the Antarctic, but he wouldn't be alone. Six men had stayed behind to continue the search, and there were plenty of supplies for the cold weather ahead. Mawson had survived.

The Unbelievable Journey

The South Pole had been captured by Roald Amundsen. Robert Falcon Scott, in his tragic effort, had also reached the pole. What was left? In 1914 Ernest Shackleton was to try an expedition that would once again put Great Britain in the leading role of polar adventurers. He proposed to land on the northwestern area of Antarctica, on the Weddell Sea, and be the first to completely cross the continent, by way of the South Pole. If he succeeded, he would have to travel some 1,800 miles, most of it in unexplored territory. The principal backer of the expedition was Sir James Caird, a wealthy businessman.

Shackleton's ship, the *Endurance,* was to proceed directly to the Weddell Sea while a second ship, the *Aurora,* would anchor at McMurdo Sound. Thousands of volunteers stepped forward for this dangerous mission, including a number of women. Shackleton picked his crew carefully, all men, and left England on August 8, 1914. The funding of the dogs was helped by money raised by British schoolchildren, and some of the dogs were named for the schools. The *Endurance* reached Antarctica in January 1915, and the crew immediately realized they were in trouble as they entered the pack ice off the Weddell Sea coast. As temperatures fell

SHACKLETON WITH CREW MEMBERS ON BOARD THE *ENDURANCE*

unexpectedly fast, the *Endurance* was soon trapped in the drifting floes, unable to maneuver under its own power. The ice was dense enough that the crew could climb overboard and exercise on the floes.

SLED DOGS WATCH AS THE *ENDURANCE* SINKS INTO PACK ICE

They had to use great caution because whales, spotting either seals or dogs, could burst through the ice and snatch them off. One whale made a hole twenty-five feet across as it went after a seal.

CREW MEMBERS TRY TO CUT A WAY THROUGH THE ICE FOR THE *ENDURANCE*

By January 19, the *Endurance* was frozen solidly in the ice. The men left the ship and set up their camp on the ice. Igloos were built to shelter the dogs. They called them "dogloos." The crew of the *Endurance* would have to spend the winter waiting to see what would happen to their ship.

In October, the Antarctic spring, the pressure of the ice against its sides caused the ship to leak badly. Crew members climbed aboard and dug through the coal in the ship's hold to try and stop the leaks. Shackleton wrote in his journal.

☙

"It is hard to write what I feel. To a sailor his ship is more than a floating home. . . . It was a sickening sensation to feel the decks breaking up under one's feet."

❧

The crew unloaded what supplies they could from the ship as they heard the boards cracking around them. Soon, the ice completely crushed the wooden ship, splintering its sides and decks. On November 21, the ship disappeared forever beneath the ice. It had been trapped in the ice for 281 days and had drifted over 570 miles from its original position. A motion picture of the *Endurance* being crushed by the ice was made by Frank Hurley, the expedition's Australian photographer. It is an interesting recording of the event, but the idea that it might have meant the deaths of all the crew members is frightening.

CREW MEMBERS UNLOAD AND SET UP BASE CAMP ON THE ICE AROUND THE *ENDURANCE*

There had been three lifeboats on the *Endurance,* and the twenty-eight-man crew began to drag them over the ice. The boats were heavy burdens to carry through snow that was as much as four feet deep. They weren't walking on land but on ice floes and knew that at any moment the ice beneath them could break.

Finally, boldly walking out toward the open sea, they saw enough space to put the lifeboats into the water. On April 12, they were

SHACKLETON AND OTHERS
LAUNCH THE *JAMES CAIRD*

still in the boats, in the Weddell Sea, headed toward Elephant Island. When the boats landed on the shore, it was the first time the men had been on solid land in sixteen months.

What were they to do? There were some penguins on the island to eat, but that diet could not sustain the men forever, and the supplies from the *Endurance* were limited. One man had suffered a heart attack and others were close to the edge. But Shackleton knew where they were, and where the nearest help would be located. On April 24, six crew members, including Shackleton, started out in the lifeboat *James Caird* for South Georgia Island, some eight hundred miles away. It was a desperate gamble but the only chance they had.

The trip was a nightmare of storms as the 23-foot boat tossed its way through the violent Antarctic water. The men, unbelievably cold and clinging desperately to the boat, had to constantly chop away the water that froze against the sides. The small sailboat made good time, sixty to seventy miles a day, but they soon discovered that only eighteen gallons of the water they carried was drinkable. Shackleton estimated one pint of water per man per day, but toward the end of the journey he was forced to cut the water ration down to a half-pint per day. Somehow, through good navigation and a lot of luck, they reached South Georgia Island on May 10, 1916.

The strong currents around the island, combined with the fierce winds, made it impossible to sail around it to the whaling stations on the north side. They were forced to travel the last distance by land.

South Georgia is a mountainous island that had not been previously crossed. On May 15, Shackleton, along with the two men still capable of going on, began the climb over the mountains. Shackleton had to fight not only the elements, but the overwhelming urge to surrender to fatigue. When the men would fall asleep he would wake them after an hour and tell them they had been asleep longer. He wanted to keep them alive. Finally, exhausted and barely alert, they arrived on the other side of the island.

Shackleton was delighted to see the workers at the whaling station. When he and his men finally made it to the station, exhausted and on the verge of desperation, the whaling men were equally shocked. There was no ship to be seen, and yet there were three men knocking on the door of the manager's villa, a two-story house with smoke curling from its chimney. Shackleton asked for tea and began to relate his miraculous story. History was being made and, luckily, history without the tinge of tragedy.

It took three more months to get the necessary supplies and a ship that could manage to get to the isolated and difficult shores of Elephant Island, where the other crew members waited. Miraculously, they had all survived the long wait for Ernest Shackleton.

BYRD BRINGS TECHNOLOGY TO ANTARCTICA

*R*oald Amundsen and Robert Falcon Scott both reached the South Pole. Ernest Shackleton's heroics trying to cross the Antarctic continent were the stuff of legend. Douglas Mawson had significantly expanded the scientific knowledge of the area. Most of the major expeditions had occurred prior to the World War I period, 1914–1918. By the time Richard Evelyn Byrd ventured to Antarctica in 1928, technology had changed considerably. There were new opportunities for exploration.

Byrd was born in Winchester, Virginia, in 1888. His family was both wealthy and influential. A flying enthusiast from an early age, he had been a flight instructor during World War I. In 1926 he and Floyd Bennett, a pilot and a personal friend of Byrd's, were the first to attempt a flight over the North Pole. Among the first to congratulate him on his efforts was Roald Amundsen. The Norwegian explorer was very much interested in the possibilities that new technologies offered.

In 1928 Byrd decided to take American technology south. He contacted Amundsen and asked him for advice. Amundsen sent Byrd a series of letters, with detailed advice on how to conquer the pole. He advised Byrd to use dogs, the best equipment, and only the best men. There was little to argue about, considering Amundsen's success. Byrd took three planes — two small ones and a large Ford plane with three engines. The planes were all adapted for flying in the high altitude and cold weather. He also took ninety-five dogs and fifty men.

In June the men received the disheartening news that Roald Amundsen had been killed in a plane accident during a rescue mission in the Arctic. Byrd sent telegrams of remorse back to the States.

Byrd's ship, the *City of New York,* left its Hoboken pier on August

THE *CITY OF NEW YORK*

25, 1928. A Norwegian-built wooden ship, it chugged through the choppy waters of the Hudson River using both sail and auxiliary steam power.

The ship was reinforced on all sides, with thicknesses as great as thirty-four inches in some areas. Being towed a great part of the way, the ship reached the Ross Ice Shelf on Christmas Day. Byrd set up his base near the Bay of Whales and called it Little America. This would soon turn out to be the largest encampment ever created in Antarctica. There were two major huts with a 600-foot tunnel between them that Byrd had lined with food supplies.

One of the first tasks assigned to the crew was to set up three tall radio towers. Byrd would be in touch with his men and with the world. In 1912 it had taken nearly a year before the world knew about Amundsen's success and Scott's tragedy. They would know of Byrd's successes or failures almost instantly. A radio connection with the *New York Times* was immediately established. Byrd's teams also used two-way radios, introducing them into the Antarctic for the first time.

On January 15, 1929, Byrd made his first Antarctic flight. Eight days later he flew over the Ross Ice Shelf, discovering a range of mountains that had not been previously seen. He named them the Rockefeller Mountains. Later, Laurence Gould, a geologist and second in command, flew with two men and landed at the base of the mountains to study them more closely. He was caught in a sudden Antarctic storm and the plane was picked up, sent flying across the ice, and destroyed by the 150-mile-per-hour gusts of

wind. Byrd, flying in the other small plane, found the three men, shaken but still alive, a few days later.

The sun set on April 19, and was followed by 125 days of darkness. The expedition team wintered over in their sophisticated digs. They took temperature, barometric, and wind velocity readings on a regular basis. Since they were connected to the world by radio, they were aware of what was going on as they huddled in their quarters. They received news of the temperatures in America, noting that one day it was 96 degrees in New York City and 72 degrees below zero in Little America.

The space they lived in was luxurious compared to the quarters of the expeditions that had preceded them. The men had brought various forms of entertainment with them, and their diets were superior to those of any previous teams. Byrd had also brought highly skilled mechanics and craftsmen with him. Some of them, to amuse themselves, made a set of Antarctic clothing for Byrd's dog Igloo. The outfit consisted of a little suit (with a hole for his tail), a fur scarf, and booties. Puppies were born to some of the dogs, and a carpenter built a miniature sledge for them to pull. When the tiny puppies were lined up in front of the sledge as if they were going to pull it, their mother came and got them one by one and returned them to the kennel. Apparently, she had no patience for such foolishness.

In October the men began to prepare for the flight over the

BYRD AND HIS CREW DRINKING COFFEE IN FRONT OF THE AIRPLANE

pole. They would fly from Little America over the Queen Maud Mountains to the pole. If the plane were to crash and the crew survive, they would be stranded hundreds of miles from the base. Depots had to be set out and sufficient food had to be carried on the plane to ensure the safe return of the four-man crew, which would include Byrd; Bert Balchen, the pilot; Harold June, the relief pilot and radio operator; and Ashley McKinley, the photographer and aerial surveyor.

The dogs, per the advice of Amundsen, were well trained and worked well with the drivers as they began to lay the supply depots. There was one sad story, though. Spy, an older lead dog who had gone lame, still wanted to lead his team. The old dog limped after the driving team, pushing his body painfully along the trail, catching up with the younger dogs only when they stopped to rest. The drivers knew he couldn't keep up very long and it would have been too cruel to allow him to starve in the polar desert. They had to take Spy aside and shoot him.

As the team laid depots along the route of the plane, they came across a cairn that had been erected years before by Amundsen. A note he left read, in part, ". . . Passed this cache on our return from South Pole with provisions for 60 days, 2 sledges, 11 dogs. All well."

Flying in the Arctic or Antarctic was difficult. Engines had to be carefully warmed before starting, for a cold engine simply would not start in the frigid temperatures. Once the engines were stopped, the oil had to be drained immediately, before it could thicken and clog the engines. Also, the three-engine Ford airplane could not carry enough fuel, along with its other supplies, to make the journey from Little America to the pole and back. So a fuel supply was left at the foot of the Queen Maud Mountains for the return trip.

A compass points to the magnetic pole, not the geographic pole. Navigating from a considerable distance away from the poles indicates the general proximity of the geographic pole. But as the compass nears the actual poles, the distance between the south magnetic pole and the south geographic pole becomes obvious. Byrd would have to use a sun compass and a sextant to try to locate the geographic pole.

On November 28, they decided to make the attempt. The plane took off at 3:29 in the afternoon with the ground crew cheering them on. The going was difficult. There were few markers on the ground that they could recognize from the air. If the plane drifted off course it could be a disaster. The plane's speed varied with the winds it encountered, but never achieved speeds much over one hundred miles per hour.

As they approached the Queen Maud Mountains, a new problem developed. The *Floyd Bennett* was loaded to its maximum and was having difficulty climbing. Could they get over the mountains? Balchen, the pilot, didn't think they were going to make it. They decided to lighten the plane's load and threw out a precious bag of food. They were going to try to go through a gap in the mountains and the plane was nosed up. The plane began to shake and Balchen yelled for them to get rid of more weight. More food was thrown out. The only thing they had left to dump was fuel. But dumping fuel might mean they wouldn't get back.

Finally, the plane began to climb again and it cleared the mountains with very little room to spare. Shortly after one o'clock in the morning of November 29, they calculated that they had reached the South Pole. Byrd had Balchen make a five-mile circle to be sure they had reached their target. They then dropped a stone wrapped in an American flag, over the pole.

On the way back they stopped at the fuel depot, refueled, and

BYRD'S EXPEDITION CELEBRATES IN FRONT OF THEIR AIRPLANE

started back again for Little America. They landed to a cheering team, having reached the South Pole in a little over sixteen hours. The same journey had taken Amundsen three months on the ground.

The *City of New York* had been sent to a warmer climate for repairs and fresh supplies. When she returned late, the base had to be hurriedly dismantled. The planes were left to the Antarctic winter. But the Byrd expedition had established the American presence on the continent. He had discovered over a quarter-million square miles of land, had found a new mountain range, and had flown over the South Pole.

In his next expedition to the Antarctic, which took place in 1933–1935, he decided to test the possibility of a scientist spending the winter at an isolated station. He chose himself to test the idea of putting a man in a sheltered, heated position to take readings during the worst part of the Antarctic winter. The generator malfunctioned, sending dangerous fumes into Byrd's small hut and nearly killing him. But Byrd survived, and eventually headed expeditions to the bottom of the world until his death in 1957.

All in all, Byrd explored by air more than any other explorer. Using the superior equipment available to him, as well as radio technology and air power, his expeditions amassed an enormous amount of precise information, photographing more terrain than all of the previous explorers had seen and using mechanized vehicles successfully for the first time.

Assuring the Future

Admiral Richard E. Byrd's expedition to the South Pole signaled the change in exploration of the earth. Modern technological changes were removing the personal heroics that had for so long marked the quest to explore the ends of the earth. Airplanes could fly over the most dangerous territory. With the invention of modern radio equipment, it was no longer necessary even to lay depots. Supplies could be airlifted to remote regions, and explorers could check in with their home bases by radios. Ships that were icebound could often be freed by icebreakers, ships specifically designed to break up polar ice. This did not remove the element of personal danger. Although an Australian study indicated that humans could adapt to cold temperatures, there were clear limits on the adaptation. A person falling into the icy waters still suffered the shock of the extreme temperature change. A person caught in the extreme Antarctic weather would still have a very short time to find shelter. Humankind had not physically improved; we were no stronger than Scott and Shackleton, no more determined than Amundsen and Mawson.

World War II stopped Antarctic exploration. At the end of the war the United States found itself in the unusual position of being the world's greatest superpower. The United States, understanding

ADMIRAL BYRD, RIGHT, DURING OPERATION HIGHJUMP

that control of the poles might one day mean control of the earth, decided that a presence in the far southern region was absolutely necessary. The result was Operation Highjump, conducted in 1946 and 1947. To a war-weary America, however, the idea of a naval expedition to Antarctica gained little support. Would another expedition be worth the cost and effort?

All of the available technology would be used on this operation. Thirteen ships, thirty-three aircraft, jeeps, tractors, and thousands of men would engage in a massive effort to prepare Americans to exist, study, and to an extent, exert a measure of control over Antarctica. The number of men alone would be

Byrd watching
over Operation
Deepfreeze

more than that of all the previous expeditions and commercial adventures combined. The mission was led by Richard E. Byrd.

Operation Highjump was a major effort by the United States Navy to advance American scientific endeavors in the Antarctic. It represented a long-term commitment to research the area, its geologic history, and the effects of low temperatures on humans and machines.

Almost ten years later, in 1955, the navy launched Operation Deepfreeze, an even larger undertaking. There were four objectives: to find bases for American scientific stations, to construct a permanent base called Little America V, to set up an airfield, and to establish two other permanent bases, McMurdo Station and the Byrd Station.

In 1957 an International Geophysical Year was declared. Known as the IGY, the "year" lasted from July 1, 1957, until December 31, 1958. The IGY represented a cooperative effort by a group of twelve nations. Scientists from around the world were invited to come to Antarctica to share the research and benefits of the area. It was from this spirit of cooperation that the Antarctic Treaty was created.

The Antarctic Treaty, first signed in December 1959, is an agreement among the original twelve nations involved in the IGY to maintain the environment of Antarctica, to share as much scientific information as possible, and to keep the area as peaceful as possible. It is the one area of the world that, by agreement, is not "owned" by any one nation. There are now more than forty Antarctic Treaty partners.

Antarctica Today

Antarctica is one of the most important areas of the world. It contains 90 percent of the world's ice and 70 percent of the world's fresh water. If the ice in Antarctica were to suddenly melt, it would raise the oceans well over one hundred feet. What happens to the Antarctic climate will clearly have an effect on the rest of the world. This is one of the reasons that the United States Antarctic Program was established in 1959.

Today there are forty-four permanent bases in the Antarctic region. During the summer months about four thousand scientists, construction workers, and support staff work in the area. This figure drops to less than one thousand in the cold winter months. Experiments that cannot be conducted anywhere else, in astronomy, atmospheric sciences, biology, glaciology, and oceanography are carried out on a regular basis. Ski-equipped planes bring in supplies, and the entire region is connected to the rest of the world through telephones, television, and the Internet. Still, the harsh regions of the area are quite dangerous.

The last regular flight into the continent occurs in late February. In June, midwinter in Antarctica, supplies can be dropped from planes. But if a serious accident were to occur during the winter months, away from one of the scientific stations, it would be difficult to get help to the victim. Recently a doctor became ill and had to wait for months before someone could reach her.

The Antarctic continent is larger than the United States and Mexico combined, primarily because of its huge ice mass. In 2003 a chunk of the ice about the size of the state of Delaware broke off. Scientists wondered what effect it would have on the continent and the rest of the world. Did it reflect a major global warming problem or was it just part of the natural evolution of Antarctica? While the temperature above the Antarctic is somewhat elevated, there has been an actual increase over the last hundred years in the amount of ice in the region.

When I visited the Arctic as a teenager in the army, I was fascinated by the fact that the earth that I thought I knew could be so different at the poles. The vast ice fields filled me with awe as the ship I was on pushed and prodded its way to higher and higher latitudes. The animals, the vegetation, the bleakness, and most of all, the numbing cold, all had an influence on me that remains until this day. I can imagine what it must have been like to be the first to travel to Antarctica. I would have loved to have been with either Scott or Amundsen trekking southward, checking my bearings against the position of the Antarctic sun as we neared the pole. I would have liked to have been the first person to have seen Mount Erebus or the Ross Ice Shelf.

The Antarctic was the last unexplored landmass on Earth, and the adventures of discovery and exploration are history now. People still challenge the elements and themselves by trekking over the frozen white desert, but with radio communication and modern transportation, they do it in relative safety. Today it is even possible to visit the Antarctic Peninsula and other areas of Antarctica as a tourist.

In January 2004, the first photographs from Mars were shown on television. They show a cold and desolate place that might once have supported some form of life. Scientists are wondering what lies beneath the surface of the red planet. Government officials are talking about the costs of an expedition. I sense how they feel. Will we someday perhaps send men to Mars? As we push into the frontiers of space and perhaps of time itself, the human sense of adventure and curiosity will prevail. Somehow the bravest of us will push on, will want to know what is beyond the next star, the next dimension, and to boldly go where no man has gone before.

FACTS ABOUT ANTARCTICA

- The area of Antarctica is 5.4 million square miles.
- 90% of the world's ice is in Antarctica.
- The average thickness of the Antarctic ice sheet is 7,090 feet.
- The Ross Ice Shelf is as big as France.
- Inland temperatures in the summer rise to *minus* 20 degrees.
- At fourteen million square kilometers, Antarctica is the fifth-largest continent. It is about 1.5 times larger than the United States.
- During the winter months the average temperature is about *minus* 75 degrees! The lowest recorded temperature in the Antarctic was minus 129.28 at the Russian station.
- 98% of the continent is covered with an ice layer that is 7,200 feet thick.
- If all the ice in Antarctica melted, seas around the world would rise by over 200 feet.
- During the summer season there are about 4,000 scientists and support staff on the continent.
- What's up with the ozone over Antarctica? The ozone layer, about ten miles above us in the stratosphere, protects us from ultraviolet rays. Pollutants from Earth help to break down the ozone level, creating thin spaces, or "holes."
- The Antarctic has crevasses, or deep "slots" that are often covered with a thin layer of snow. Some of these crevasses can be 30 to 40 feet wide, over 40 feet deep, and virtually invisible to a traveler.
- There are valleys in Antarctica where scientists believe it has not rained for two million years. There is little rain in any part of Antarctica; it's just too cold.
- During the Antarctic winter the sea ice expands by around 40,000 square miles per day.
- Frostbite depends on exposure and temperature. At extreme temperatures frostbite (meaning that the flesh actually freezes) can begin in less than a minute.

Timeline

JANUARY 17, 1773	James Cook crosses the Antarctic Circle
JANUARY 30, 1774	James Cook reaches 71° 10' — Furthest south
FEBRUARY 19, 1819	William Smith discovers the South Shetlands
JANUARY 27, 1820	Fabian Von Bellingshausen sights the continental ice shelf
JANUARY 16, 1840	Charles Wilkes reaches Antarctica
JANUARY 9, 1841	James Clark Ross enters the Ross Sea
JANUARY 24, 1895	Borchgrevink lands on the Antarctic continent
FEBRUARY 15, 1898	The *Belgica* crosses the Antarctic Circle
JANUARY 3, 1902	Robert Falcon Scott reaches Antarctica
NOVEMBER 2, 1902	Scott begins first try for the South Pole, but fails
OCTOBER 29, 1908	Ernest Shackleton begins his try for the pole, but fails
OCTOBER 19, 1911	Amundsen starts for pole

NOVEMBER 1, 1911	Scott starts for pole
DECEMBER 14, 1911	Amundsen reaches the South Pole
JANUARY 17, 1912	Scott reaches the pole
MARCH 29, 1912	Probable deaths of Scott and his remaining crew
DECEMBER 14, 1912	Douglas Mawson's expedition runs into trouble
DECEMBER 30, 1914	Shackleton crosses the Antarctic Circle in the *Endurance*
NOVEMBER 21, 1915	The *Endurance,* crushed, sinks in the pack ice
APRIL 24, 1916	Shackleton heads for South Georgia
DECEMBER 9, 1928	Richard E. Byrd reaches Antarctica
NOVEMBER 29, 1929	Byrd flies over the South Pole
MARCH 28, 1934	Byrd alone at Bolling Advance Weather Station
AUGUST 11, 1934	Byrd is rescued from station
DECEMBER 1, 1959	Antarctic Treaty signed in Washington, D.C.

BIBLIOGRAPHY

Books

Amundsen, Roald; *South Pole, The Norwegian Antarctic Expedition in the* Fram, *1910–1912*; Cooper Square Press New York; 2001 (original 1913)

Borchgrevink, C. E.; *First on the Antarctic Continent, an Account of the British Antarctic Expedition, 1898–1900*; McGill-Queen's University Press, Montreal; 1980 (original 1901)

British Polar Expedition; *The PolarBook*; E. Allom, London; 1930

Chapman, Walker; *The Loneliest Continent*; New York Graphic Society; 1964

Cherry-Garrard, Apsley; *The Worst Journey in the World*; Picador, London (original 1922)

Evans, Edward R. G. R.; *South with Scott*; Collins, London; 1952 (original 1938)

Honnywill, Eleanor; *The Challenge of Antarctica*; Anthony Nelson, Oswerstry; 1984

Lansing, Alfred; *Endurance, Shackleton's Incredible Voyage*; Carroll & Graf, New York; 1959

Murray, George; *Antarctic Manual for the Use of the Expedition of 1901*; Royal Geographical Society, London; 1901

Naveen, Ron, Colin Monteath, Tui De Roy, and Mark Jones; *Wild Ice, Antarctic Journeys*; Smithsonian Institution Press, Washington, D.C.; 1990

Neider, Charles; *Antarctica, Authentic Accounts of Life and Exploration*; Allen & Unwin, London; 1973

Ponting, Herbert G.; *The Great White South*; Duckworth, London; 1935

Porter, Eliot; *Antarctica*; E. P. Dutton, New York; 1978 (Photobook)

Reader's Digest; *Antarctica, The Extraordinary History of Man's Conquest of the Frozen Continent*; Reader's Digest, Australia; 1985

Rubin, Jeff; *Antarctica — Travel Survival Kit*; Lonely Planet, Sydney; 1996

Scott, Robert; *Scott's Last Journey*; John Murray, London; 1935

Scott, Robert, edited by Peter King; *Scott's Last Journey*; HarperCollins, New York; 1999 (ill.)

Seaver, George; *Edward Wilson of the Antarctic*; John Murray, London; 1933 (reprint 1950)

Shackleton, Ernest; *The Heart of the Antarctic — Being the Story of the British Antarctic Expedition, 1907–1909*; Robinson Publishing, London — Carroll & Graf; 1999

Shackleton, Ernest; *South, Journals of His Last Expedition to Antarctica 1914–1917*; Konecky & Konecky, New York; 1920

Sobel, Dava; *Longitude, The True Story of a Lone Genius Who Solved the Greatest Scientific Problem of His Time*; Penguin, New York; 1995

Stewart, John; *Antarctica, An Encyclopedia*; McFarland & Co., Jefferson, North Carolina; 1990

Stonehouse, Bernard; *North Pole — South Pole, A Guide to the Ecology and Resources of the Arctic and Antarctic*; Prion, London; 1990

Weddell, James; *A Voyage Towards the South Pole, Performed in the Years 1822–24; Containing an Examination of the Antarctic Sea (1927)* David & Charles Reprints, Devon, England; 1827 (reprint 1970)

Wilkes, Charles; *Narrative of the United States' Exploring Expedition (1838, 1839, 1841, 1842)*; Whittaker & Co., London; 1845

Exhibits

South: The Race to the South Pole; National Maritime Museum; September/2000– September/2001; brochure

Illustration Credits

England; Page 94: © Hulton-Deutsch Collection/Corbis; Page 98: Hulton/Archive by Getty Images; Page 100: © Underwood & Underwood/Corbis; Page 101: The Royal Geographical Society, London; Page 102: © Hulton-Deutsch Collection/Corbis; Page 103: © Corbis; Page 106: Collection of the author; Page 108: © Keystone View Company, No. 32725; Page 110: © Keystone View Company, No. 192—(33158) Geographic Unit; Page 111: From "With Byrd at the South Pole" © 1930 Paramount Public Corporation; Page 114: From "With Byrd at the South Pole" © 1930 Paramount Public Corporation; Page 116: © Bettman/Corbis; Page 118: © Bettman/Corbis; Page 120: © Ann Hawthorne/Corbis.

Index